Dr and Mrs. Norman Wiggins,

Jocelyn R. Mosley
Dec 1, 1995

Very best wishes!
Sara Vander Clute
Dec. 1, 1995

Fayetteville
North Carolina

A City of Cultures
with a Southern Accent

Text by Sara VanderClute

Photography by Rozlyn R. Masley

LONGSTREET PRESS
ATLANTA, GEORGIA

Published in cooperation with
THE FAYETTEVILLE CHAMBER OF COMMERCE

Published by
LONGSTREET PRESS, INC.,
a subsidiary of Cox Newspapers
a subsidiary of Cox Enterprises, Inc.
2140 Newmarket Parkway
Suite 118
Marietta, Georgia 30067

Printed in the United States of America

1st printing, 1996
Library of Congress
Catalog Number 95-77261

ISBN: 1-56352-266-7

This book was printed by
Quebecor/Kingsport, Tennessee.

Color separation and film preparation
by Advertising Technologies, Inc.,
Atlanta, Georgia.

DIRECTOR, ENTERPRISE DIVISION
Nancy Bauer

MANAGING EDITOR
Erica Fox

ART DIRECTION AND PRODUCTION
Graham & Company Graphics, Inc.,
Atlanta, Georgia

Fayetteville

North Carolina

TABLE OF

C O N T E N T S

FOREWORD

ayetteville, North Carolina, is an up-and-coming city that combines elements of international élan and East Coast sophistication with the traditionally genteel ambience of the South. It's a wonderful place to live, to work, and to bring up a family, as its residents well know. Fayetteville's ideal location, its temperate climate, and its solid economic base are among the city's many merits.

But it's the people who live here who make Fayetteville the extraordinary place it is. People who were born here, people who came from elsewhere, people who speak with a southern drawl, people whose accent can't quite be pinpointed, people who fly airplanes, people who leap from them—the population of Fayetteville is a blend of absolutely fascinating people. They come together with their various and diverse talents, skills, experiences, and propensities, and somehow, by simply going about their various lives, make Fayetteville the kind of place one doesn't want to leave. It's impossible to count how many Fayettevillians arrived on the scene for what they thought would be a temporary stay and have yet to depart. They linger, and they are legion.

The pride Fayetteville has come to feel about itself and its bright future is evident. The city has come to be known by other cities across the state and region as a place where great things are happening. There's a synergy at work in Fayetteville, resulting in coordinated and cooperative efforts between business and government, true public-private partnerships. Real and measurable progress is being made in the areas of education, beautification, invigoration of the city center, leadership development, the city's ties with the military communities of Fort Bragg and Pope Air Force Base, and many other areas of common community interest.

The Fayetteville Chamber of Commerce is proud to represent Fayetteville's diverse and growing business community. The Chamber has become a strong and effective force for good in the community and can say with informed certainty that Fayetteville's future is bright. By 1999, when the Chamber will celebrate its centennial anniversary, Fayetteville will be even closer to achieving its destiny as a center of business and culture within the region.

The Fayetteville Chamber of Commerce is eager to acquaint you with this remarkable community. Read about, and see in these wonderful photographs, the people and places that make Fayetteville, North Carolina, *A City of Cultures with a Southern Accent.*

FAYETTEVILLE CHAMBER OF COMMERCE

INTRODUCTION

■ *The annual production of "The Nutcracker" by the Dance Theatre of Fayetteville, staged annually at Methodist College, is a delight for children of all ages.*

Fayetteville, North Carolina's fourth-largest metropolitan area, is a city that cannot be characterized in one simple phrase. Firmly planted in a setting that is 24-karat southern, Fayetteville is much like a multifaceted jewel. Sparkling with the cultures and customs of far-flung nations, but imbued with the finest of southern traditions, Fayetteville is indeed a city of cultures with a southern accent.

But the cultures flourishing in Fayetteville are not merely those of other nations; the culture of commerce, the military culture with its proud traditions, Fayetteville's contemporary culture, as well as its cultured past, and the quiet culture of caring that serves as Fayetteville's conscience are all part of the fabulous gem of a city that is Fayetteville.

Certainly a military town, Fayetteville is proud to be the home of Fort Bragg and Pope Air Force Base (AFB). International events often focus the world's attention on this vital military complex. When that happens, Fayetteville's pride in the men and women who wear the uniform is especially heartfelt, for

they are our friends, our neighbors, our customers, and our family.

Though the military connection may be the most well-known facet of Fayetteville's identity, it is only one part of the city's complex character. Fayetteville also has an ever-growing business community that includes many nationally and internationally known industrial and manufacturing companies.

Fayetteville is also a college town. Considering the accessibility of the colleges and universities in town or within an easy commute, it's easy to understand why Fayetteville is a community of lifelong learners.

The cultural benefits of being a college town are freely available to the greater community. When the Alvin Ailey Dance Company makes an appearance at Fayetteville State University, the audience is made up of people from across the region. Likewise, when Methodist College's drama department stages a production, people from the greater community are in the audience.

Fayetteville, as a community, greatly appreciates the arts. It is home to many talented artists, visual

■ *Fayetteville is a great place to raise a family. It is also a great place to pursue an education and to do business. Fayetteville State University (upper right) is one of several area colleges, and ICI (lower right), which produces fiber, is one of many thriving businesses. And wherever you go, there is a feeling of hospitality, as symbolized by the pineapple.*

and performing, but it is the accessibility of the arts that makes Fayetteville such a stimulating place to live. A vibrant arts community, sustained in some measure by the commitment of local businesses and government, works hard to promote the arts as a quality-of-life issue. An exhibit, a performance, a reading, a display, or a play is on the community calendar almost any day of the year, tempting the resident or visitor who wants to be touched by the arts, in one form or another.

At the same time, it would be misleading to characterize Fayetteville as just an uptown girl. Fayetteville wears blue jeans, too. The crowds at the Monster Truck Rally, in the civic center arena, are as large and enthusiastic as at the city's more sedate offerings. You'll find as enthusiastic a crowd at any high school or college ball game, cheering for the home team, as you will at an opening-night gala at the Cape Fear Regional Theater. Be it ball games and beer or black tie and bubbly, one can find one's niche in Fayetteville.

Scots settled Fayetteville more than two centuries ago. Now, Fayetteville is home to people of diverse ethnic backgrounds, nationalities, and experiences. This marvelous amalgam of people gives Fayetteville a cosmopolitan flavor, which, when combined with traditional southern customs and courtesies, makes it truly a city of cultures with a southern accent.

With its rich history and a future full of potential, Fayetteville is moving toward the twenty-first century with great enthusiasm. The community commitment to building a city that is hospitable to resident and visitor alike, one imbued with a healthy economic environment that encourages growth and prosperity, is evident. Those who have come to love Fayetteville know it is a great place to live, to work, to raise a family. But, to borrow a phrase from our Army neighbors, we want to be all that we can be. Fulfilling that potential is an exciting way to spend the last decade of the twentieth century.

■ *Fayetteville is a city with a strong identity. The Scottish influence is very apparent, as is the presence of Fort Bragg and Pope Air Force Base. Members of the Army's Golden Knights parachute team (**right**), which is stationed at Fort Bragg, put on demonstrations across the country.*

THE PLACE,
THE PEOPLE

■ *When the occasion calls for dining out, people in
Fayetteville can choose from a veritable smorgasbord
of authentic international cuisines.*

■ *Street festivals offer a wonderful opportunity to sample the cultures of other nations and ethnic groups in Fayetteville. You may marvel at Filipinos performing a cane dance (**upper left**), admire the colorful native dress of Panama, or interact with people from halfway around the world.*

To find Fayetteville on a map, find the Outer Banks on the Atlantic shore, locate the southern part of Pamlico Sound, and move your finger directly west. Fayetteville is about a third of the way across North Carolina—tantalizingly close to the pristine beaches that make up the state's Atlantic shoreline yet within a few hours' drive of the mountainous western regions of North Carolina.

Fayetteville is technically a part of the area known as the Sandhills, which is neither as hilly as the Piedmont region of North Carolina nor as low and wet as the more coastal region of the state. The Cape Fear River makes its way through the city as it flows to the Atlantic Ocean near Wilmington. Known early on by the settlers in this region as the Charles River, the Cape Fear got its intriguing name because of the treacherous shoals at its mouth, as well as the fearsome pirates that occasionally plied those waters.

Today, the Cape Fear River is less significant to Fayetteville than

Interstate 95, which intersects the city, connecting the northernmost reaches of Maine with Miami. Fayetteville is just about the halfway point for the New Yorkers, New Englanders, and Canadians who make the long drive each year to Florida. Interstate 73, connecting Detroit to Charleston, South Carolina, is slated to pass just south of Fayetteville and will bring with it an increased flow of travelers, commerce, and tourism dollars to the region.

Travel east and west from Fayetteville is also easy. The city is just slightly south of Benson, where Interstate 95 intersects with Interstate 40, which connects the east and west coasts of America. I-40 makes travel to the southern beaches fast and convenient, as well as trips west to the mountains.

Fayetteville is about an hour's drive from Raleigh, the state capital. The charming port city of Wilmington is about a two-hour drive; from Fayetteville to Asheville is just five hours, if one can resist

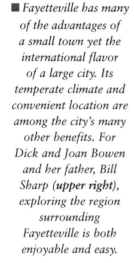

■ *Fayetteville has many of the advantages of a small town yet the international flavor of a large city. Its temperate climate and convenient location are among the city's many other benefits. For Dick and Joan Bowen and her father, Bill Sharp (upper right), exploring the region surrounding Fayetteville is both enjoyable and easy.*

ACCORDING TO A CENTRAL MICHIGAN UNIVERSITY STUDY, FAYETTEVILLE IS ONE OF THE MOST INTEGRATED CITIES IN AMERICA.

There are plenty of ways to have fun in Fayetteville. Many people enjoy dancing, outside at a street festival or at the many nightspots in town. Others, especially children, enjoy taking a ride along the Cape Fear River.

the temptation to stop and explore the many furniture outlets throughout the North Carolina towns of Greensboro, Hickory, and Morganton. Interstate travelers will find Fayetteville is also an easy day's drive from Washington, D.C., and Atlanta.

Fayetteville's enviable geographical location is what gives it one of its most often-mentioned advantages—the moderate climate. Blessed with distinct seasons, Fayetteville is spared the brutal extremes of winter and summer. It can be warm and humid in the summer, but when the snows fly in Boston and Buffalo, Fayettevillians are often out on the golf course.

The transitional seasons of spring and autumn are mild and lovely, each with an array of colors. Breathtaking azaleas, dogwoods, and flowering bulbs bloom everywhere in the spring. And come fall, the leaves of the diverse hardwoods lend a golden aura that makes Fayettevillians grateful they can call Fayetteville home.

A HEALTHY MIX OF PEOPLE

Fayetteville's population is composed of a healthy mix of ethnic, racial, and cultural groups. In the mid-1990s, the greater Fayetteville population, including Fort Bragg and Pope AFB, was 292,276; by the year 2010, it's expected to approach 330,000.

Fayetteville is a youthful community. The median age is 27.8 years, lower than the state or national figure. In 1993, more than half of Fayetteville's population was between the ages of 18 and 49; only 16.7 percent were older than 50.

The youthfulness of Fayetteville's population is influenced by the military presence and contributes positively to the community's overall complexion. The population mix can be expected to change a bit as more and more people choose Fayetteville as a retirement home and the American population in general ages.

According to 1990 figures from the U.S. Census of Population and Housing, Fayetteville is 62 percent white, 32 percent black, and 6 percent "other." The military influence may well be responsible for another feature of Fayetteville's residential life. According to a study done at Central Michigan University, published in *American Demographics* in September 1992, Fayetteville is the fourth least-segregated suburban community in America. According to the study, cities with a high percentage of military population are likely to have residential areas that are highly integrated. (Jacksonville, North Carolina, is the least segregated city, followed by Lawton, Oklahoma; the most segregated city, according to the study, is Gary, Indiana.)

A Stable, Hard-Working Community

Fayettevillians are a hard-working group; the area's unemployment rate is normally between 4 and 6.5 percent. With a labor force of about 112,000, and growing every year, the expansion of existing businesses, and the influx of new industry, Fayettevillians are assured of work for some time to come.

People in Fayetteville have put their disposable income to good use, contributing to the phenomenal growth of the retail sector in the past decade. Food store sales increased by 75 percent in that time, food and drink sales by 140 percent, automobile sales by 139 percent, and drugstore sales by a whopping 221 percent.

Although Fayetteville cannot be characterized as a wealthy community, it has a stable economic base, and the number of households with an annual income of $50,000 or more is rising. Statistics show that the percentage with annual incomes of less than $20,000 is decreasing.

For Fayettevillians, the future is increasingly bright. They know that while they are working hard, and playing with equal enthusiasm, progress is being made on many fronts. Fayetteville is truly coming into its own, and those who have known for decades what a fine place it is to work, to live, and to bring up a family are delighted to know that the rest of the world is beginning to see that as well.

A CULTURED PAST

■ Cool Spring Tavern housed some of the delegates to the 1789
North Carolina General Assembly, at which the U.S. Constitution was
ratified. The tavern is now used as lawyers' offices.

■ *The Market House, which houses the offices of the Olde Fayetteville Association, has a long and fascinating history.*

The city of Fayetteville has a fascinating history, in part because it has been the setting for some of the most significant moments in North Carolina's history.

The result of a merger of two early Scottish settlements along the Cape Fear River, Campbellton and Cross Creek, Fayetteville was known before 1783 as Upper and Lower Campbellton. In that year, the North Carolina General Assembly authorized the name to be changed to Fayetteville, as a tribute to the Marquis de Lafayette, the French nobleman who had been so helpful to the colonies in achieving independence. Fayetteville was the first town to demonstrate an admiration for the marquis in this way, and, it is said, the only such town that the marquis visited, which he did in 1825.

Many structures in Fayetteville withstood the tumultuous events of the 1700s and 1800s. Among them are Cool Spring Tavern, on Cool Spring Street, which once functioned as the lodging place for visitors to Fayetteville and is now the offices of a law firm; Barges Tavern, a small wooden structure, dating from the late 1700s, which is now the Barges Tavern Conference Center for the Fayetteville Chamber of Commerce; and the Market House, a handsome structure built to replace the State House, which burned in the Great Fire of 1831.

The loss of the State House was lamentable, for it was in that building, in November 1789, that the North Carolina General Assembly voted to adopt and ratify the United States Constitution. Why in Fayetteville, one might ask. Because it served as the state capital four times between 1788 and 1793. Many thought Fayetteville should be chosen as the permanent capital, but it lost out—by one vote—to the general assembly's choice, in Wake County, to what became the city of Raleigh.

The General Assembly took other significant action in Fayetteville in November 1789, including establishing the charter of the University of North Carolina (which in 1795 became the first state university to begin operation); ceding the westernmost section of North Carolina to the federal government (this ultimately became a part of Tennessee); and issuing the orders for the construction of a lighthouse on Ocracoke Island, to protect seagoing vessels. The lighthouse also has served for years as a scenic landmark for the state.

THE MARKET HOUSE

There is no doubt that the Great Fire of 1831, which has been likened to Chicago's great conflagration, was devastating to Fayetteville. The fire, which was of unknown causes, began at about noon on Sunday, May 29, and destroyed every business in town, as well as 600 homes.

The very next year, the Market House was built on the site of the former State House, and it has since served as a public marketplace, a library, a bank, a church meeting place, a town hall, an art museum, and a museum of history. It currently houses the offices of the Olde Fayetteville Association.

In 1989, the Market House was the center of a controversy when Fayetteville celebrated the bicentennial anniversary of North Carolina's ratification of the U.S. Constitution. Many of the celebratory events centered around the Market House, because it stood where the State House had been when the state's ratification

■ *Reenactments show Fayettevillians and visitors what life was like in the camps during the Civil War. These buildings are on the grounds of the Fair Oaks estate, which was the site of General Sherman's encampment.*

THE GREAT FIRE OF 1831, WHICH HAS BEEN LIKENED TO CHICAGO'S GREAT FIRE, WAS DEVASTATING TO FAYETTEVILLE. EVERY BUSINESS IN TOWN WAS DESTROYED AND 600 HOMES.

took place. In fact, the North Carolina General Assembly had agreed to hold a commemorative session in Fayetteville, in April 1989, as part of the year-long series of celebratory events.

When it came time to hold the session, however, the Black Caucus of the general assembly voted to boycott it. The fact that in the 1800s the Market House had been the setting for the sales and the division of property that included slaves was offensive to members of the caucus.

Only one member of the caucus, Senator C. R. Edwards of Fayetteville, chose to participate in the special session. On a glorious April morning, on the very site where his ancestors might have been considered property, Edwards took his place as an elected official of the North Carolina General Assembly.

The local controversy about the Market House was ultimately resolved later in 1989, when the Fayetteville City Council decided to place a plaque in the building. That plaque, which now hangs in the newly renovated structure, is inscribed with a quotation from a work by Charles Waddell Chesnutt, a prolific black writer, who was born in Fayetteville in 1858: "We shall come up slowly and painfully perhaps, but we shall win our way."

The following text is inscribed under the quotation:

In memory and honor of those indomitable people who were stripped of their dignity when sold as slaves at this place. Their courage in that time is a proud heritage of all times. They endured the past so the future could be won for freedom and justice. Their suffering and shame

afforded the opportunity for future generations to be responsible citizens, free to live, work and worship in the pursuit of the blessings of liberty to ourselves and our posterity.

With that statement, both the black and white communities of Fayetteville put the Market House controversy behind them.

THE FAYETTEVILLE ARSENAL

In the Civil War years, Fayetteville held a position of some importance because the federal government authorized an arsenal to be built there. During the events leading up to North Carolina's secession from the Union, in May 1861, the arsenal was taken over by troops sympathetic to the Confederacy. In the last two years of the Civil War, it is said that the Fayetteville arsenal was a frantic hive of activity where more than 500 workers churned out rockets, fuses, and guns.

In fact, it was the tempting prospect of destroying the arsenal that drew General William T. Sherman to Fayetteville in March 1865. Much of the arsenal's cache of weapons had been hidden before his arrival, but in spite of, or perhaps because of this fact, General Sherman burned the arsenal to the ground. In John A. Oates's historic tome, *The Story of Fayetteville*, he writes of the "angry flames . . . creating terrific heat, great pillars of black smoke darkening the heavens . . . loaded shells exploding continuously, creating the impression of a heavy artillery engagement."

The destruction of the arsenal and, at the same time, the burning of the offices of the *Fayetteville Observer* foretold the end of the war, which occurred just one month later. Because so much devastation was

■ *The arsenal grounds, which are now a part of the Museum of the Cape Fear.*

■ *Designated an All-America*
City by the National Municipal
League in 1985, Fayetteville
blends a strong sense of history
with a patriotic spirit. Events
from the Revolutionary War
and the Civil War are reenacted
*throughout the area (**above**), and*
the military is honored in events
like Operation Celebration,
which welcomed home soldiers
from the Gulf War.

unleashed on Fayetteville, some Fayettevillians still choose to refer to the Civil War as the War of Northern Aggression.

FORT BRAGG AND POPE AIR FORCE BASE

The stage was set for Fayetteville's more recent history in 1918 when the U.S. Army, in search of an appropriate place for an artillery firing center, acquired about 122,000 acres northwest of Fayetteville. Known initially as Camp Bragg, in honor of Braxton Bragg, an artillery general who served in the Confederate Army, the post has become home to some of the U.S. Army's finest fighting forces.

General William J. Snow, the artillery general who first instigated the survey of what is now Fort Bragg, could hardly have known that someday the post, and the troops who train and serve there, would figure prominently in world events. He would probably be proud that in 1994, knowing that Fort Bragg's 82D Airborne Division was en route to Haiti, the military junta on the island would agree to leave peacefully and permit the return of President Jean-Bertrand Aristide.

Fort Bragg and Pope Air Force Base have come to define Fayetteville in a way that makes residents of the city rightfully proud. In the urgent buildup of forces during World War II, it was difficult to absorb the many soldiers who were arriving, although even then Fayetteville residents opened their homes and their hearts to many a soldier and many a soldier's bride.

Fayetteville supported its soldiers and airmen in subsequent military actions, including the Vietnam War. To Fayetteville, these young men and women are not faceless strangers but friends and family who follow orders to defend America's interests wherever that may take them, whether it's the Dominican Republic, Panama, Vietnam, Iran, or Saudi Arabia.

The Gulf War period, in the early 1990s, when so many of America's troops were in Saudi Arabia protecting against further invasion into the region by Iraq's military forces, was an especially trying and frightening time for Fayetteville. As one might expect, the prolonged absence of so many troops from Fort Bragg and Pope Air Force Base, and the subsequent departure of many of their families, had an adverse effect on the local economy. But local support for the troops never wavered. Fayettevillians waited, hoped, and prayed for the hostilities to end, but only with victory over Saddam Hussein's forces.

When the war did end and the troops returned to America, the Fayetteville community staged a huge welcome-home rally, dubbed Operation Celebration, to demonstrate its pride in its military communities. That celebration, which was both joyous and memorable, was the forerunner to the now-annual Operation Appreciation, an annual "thank you" to the city's military neighbors for all they do for Fayetteville, all the time, not just during a crisis.

A KALEIDOSCOPE OF CULTURES

■ *Kilts and names beginning with Mc and Mac reflect the influence of the Scots on Fayetteville today.*

A look through the Fayetteville telephone directory reveals pages of names beginning with *Mc* and *Mac* that are undeniably Scottish in origin. This is but one example of the influence of the Scottish settlers in the valley of the Cape Fear River on Fayetteville today.

There are also more kilts per capita in Fayetteville than in almost any other American city—and they are much in evidence any time the city celebrates. When the Cape Fear Valley Clan goes proudly marching down the street, kilts swinging, accompanied by the stirring music of the bagpipes and drums of the Cross Creek Pipes and Drums, many spectators who aren't Scottish wish they were.

But more than just the Scottish influence is evident in Fayetteville. The city has acquired and absorbed people of many nationalities, ethnicities, and cultures. In fact, Fayetteville may well be the most international city in North Carolina. As many as 38 nationalities are thought to be represented among Fayetteville's population, including Turkish, Finnish, and Ukrainian.

INTERNATIONAL FOLK FESTIVAL

There's nothing *faux* or *ersatz* about Fayetteville's international offerings. At the annual International Folk Festival, an early autumn event, visitors can experience the food and music of many nations, while mingling with people from around the world. This grand party, bigger and better every year, got its start in the early 1970s when Dr. Sid Gautam, a native of India, and the late Connie Rabano, who long led the Philippine-American Club, organized a program of ethnic performances. These days, the festival is a swirl of colorful sights, rhythmic sounds, and succulent foods that combine to make it a memorable celebration of diversity yet one that is unifying as well.

The smiling gentleman behind the counter at the Hay Street Shoe Shop, and his lovely wife, who sometimes helps out in the business, have quite a tale to tell. Happily at home in Fayetteville now, they are Vietnamese by birth.

Mrs. Pham remembers vividly the 29th of April 1975. That's when her brother, a Vietnamese naval officer who was fleeing the country after the fall of Saigon to Viet Cong forces, gathered up the Phams and transported the entire family to the Philippines by boat. Once they arrived there, they were asked by American authorities if they had any American contacts who might sponsor their immigration into America.

"I knew Admiral Elmo Zumwalt, Jr.," Mrs. Pham recalls. "I had escorted Mrs. Zumwalt when she was visiting Saigon, and I hoped that the admiral would remember us."

He did. Not long after their arrival in the Philippines, Admiral Zumwalt placed a call to the Phams, assuring them that he would help expedite their immigration to America.

"You were kind and helpful to me," Mrs. Pham recalls him saying. "Now it's my turn to help you."

Just as the Phams were scheduled to fly to the Zumwalt home in the Washington, D.C., area, Admiral Zumwalt contacted them to say his home was full with other Vietnamese refugees. He asked them to travel to his son's home in Fayetteville, North Carolina, which they did. Elmo Zumwalt III was then a young attorney in Fayetteville, and he opened his home to the Pham family. They've been in Fayetteville ever since.

Martha Duell, who is French by birth, is the widow of an American Army officer. She has called Fayetteville home for many years and has come to be one of its more vocal and visible advocates, but she has never relinquished her French identity. Instrumental in establishing the LaFayette Society in 1981, a group of local Francophiles that functions as a loyal "fan club" of the Marquis de Lafayette, Martha Duell travels often to France but invariably returns "home" to Fayetteville.

"I have two countries to love," says Martha Duell, acknowledging her devotion to her native France and her adopted home of America. That same passion extends to

■ *Downtown street festivals attract people from around the world, like this Nigerian family or these members of a French touring group, who came to the Dogwood Festival. Fayetteville even has its own Eiffel Tower, in the Bordeaux Shopping Center (right).*

Fayetteville, and she has been a tireless advocate, both here and abroad, for the city.

"In France, they call me the ambassadress of Fayetteville," she says with a laugh. Duell travels often to France, and while there, she spreads the good word about her American hometown. She often plays hostess to French visitors to Fayetteville, be they military exchange officers or international tourists who are curious about the South. The lovely garden in the rear of her home is so carefully tended it has come to be known to the visiting French as "Le Parc."

It is because of Martha Duell's dual passion for Fayetteville and all things French that the city of Saint Avold, in the Lorraine region of France, was named a sister city to Fayetteville in 1994.

On July 4, 1995, Duell was in Paris, as the guest of the Conte René de Chambrun, a descendant of the Marquis de Lafayette. As the champagne flowed, and the toasts to the memory of the marquis were made, Duell was there, advocating Fayetteville in French—with perhaps just a touch of a southern accent.

■ *Mike and Ela Mishra,
from India, are among
many people who have
come to Fayetteville
from other parts of the
world. The Mishras
manage a local motel.*

INTERNATIONAL COMMUNITY

More than two dozen international
clubs are active in the Fayetteville
community. Whether the newcomers are from the Philippines,
France, Nepal, or Nigeria, there's a
group waiting to greet and help
assimilate them.

As one might expect, given the
military influence in Fayetteville,
many members of Fayetteville's
international community are from
Europe. During the military buildup
of World War II, Fayetteville welcomed a number of war brides, many
of them from overseas.

Many other residents of
Fayetteville arrived as World War I-era
brides from Germany, Holland, and
Belgium—or became the spouse of a
soldier or airman who came to
Fayetteville to serve at Fort Bragg or
Pope Air Force Base. (And these days,
it's possible, and not uncommon, for
the soldier to be a woman and the
European spouse her husband!)

Another large segment of
Fayetteville's international population is Southeast Asian. Of the
many Vietnamese, Korean, Thai,
and Cambodian families in
Fayetteville, some have connections
to a U.S. military sponsor, and
many located here with the help of
refugee placement organizations.
Some of these refugees fled Vietnam
or Cambodia after the war and have
gradually assisted their extended
families, left behind in Southeast
Asia, to do likewise.

The fastest-growing segment of
Fayetteville's international community is Hispanic. People from Panama,
Puerto Rico, Costa Rica, and other
points south have come to
Fayetteville, taken a look around,
and found the community receptive
to people from other places.

There's a weekly Spanish-language show on the local cable system, and another station carries a
variety of Spanish-language programming for a good part of the
broadcast day.

BUSINESS BENEFITS FROM CULTURAL DIVERSITY

The cultural diversity in Fayetteville is having a significant effect on its business community. New businesses that cater to one or another ethnic or national group are springing up with increasing frequency. Sustained by grateful and loyal customers who yearn for the special music or foodstuffs, clothing, or reading material of their native countries, these businesses are following one of the basic rules for a successful business: identify the market and meet the customers' needs.

If entrepreneurs have taken note of Fayetteville's ethnic populations, so too has the state of North Carolina. In locating the North Carolina Foreign Language Center in Fayetteville, the state acknowledged that Fayetteville has the greatest concentration of multilingual residents in the state. The center has thousands of volumes in many languages and maintains periodicals from several countries.

AFRICAN-AMERICANS

Of course, not only foreigners contribute to Fayetteville's cultural and ethnic mix. African-Americans also contribute to Fayetteville's unique character.

African-Americans make up about 30 percent of the greater Fayetteville population, and, although most are American-born, the Afrocentric aspects of their culture represent a rich part of life in Fayetteville.

The fast-paced and exciting step shows, staged by one of the step clubs or fraternities at Fayetteville State University, a traditionally black school, or the joyous sounds of any of the many black gospel choirs in Fayetteville, or the festivities associated with Kwanzaa, the African-American winter holiday, are all uniquely African-American, a blending of rhythms from a distant motherland with the experiences of this homeland, and all are a part of the kaleidoscope of life in Fayetteville, North Carolina.

■ *Hispanics are the fastest-growing segment of Fayetteville's international community. Fayetteville's many parades provide an opportunity for Mexican children to march proudly in the costumes of their native land.*

CONTEMPORARY CULTURE: THE ARTS IN FAYETTEVILLE

■ *During the summer, Fayettevillians and visitors can enjoy outdoor concerts at the Museum of Art or perhaps watch Charlotte Lane demonstrate oil painting at the Botanical Garden.*

■ *Fayetteville celebrates the arts in a variety of locations, including the Arts Center, whose stained glass windows were created by local artist Soni Martin; the Fayetteville Museum of Art, where children enjoy feeding the ducks after viewing the exhibits inside; and Fayetteville State University, whose choral group performs regularly.*

ayetteville is a city blessed with an appreciation of the arts, and there are many talented artists to satisfy the demand.

ARTS COUNCIL

The Arts Council functions as an umbrella agency that nurtures and promotes as many as 50 artistic groups in the greater Fayetteville community. From poetry and pottery to photography and painting, there is a group of Fayetteville artists working in the art form.

Located on Hay Street in Fayetteville's city center, the Arts Council is housed in a beautiful old building that once served as a U.S. post office and later as a library. Now the public rooms serve as galleries for the work of local artists. Stopping by the Arts Center, as the site is also known, to admire the photography, or the painting, or the weaving skills of a local artist can provide a quiet break in a busy day.

FAYETTEVILLE MUSEUM OF ART

Another place where one can contemplate the work of talented artists is the Fayetteville Museum of Art. The only art museum in the state designed specifically to serve as a gallery, the museum is a veritable jewel tucked away in a quiet location not far from one of Fayetteville's busy shopping areas. In the course of a year, the museum features several exhibitions, including the work of the finest North Carolina artists, as well as work by other artists. Always beautifully displayed, the exhibits rival those in larger museums, in larger cities.

In the summer, the museum sponsors a series of outdoor picnic concerts. What could be more lovely than to recline on the lush grass of the museum grounds,

moved by the strains of Vivaldi, as one gazes at the resident ducks gliding along the pond.

CAPE FEAR STUDIOS

For those who are not content merely to appreciate art but who must possess the objet d'art that captures their fancy, a visit to the Cape Fear Studios is a must. Here one can admire, or purchase, or commission a work of art.

A cooperative effort among local artists, the Cape Fear Studios serves as a common meeting place for artists and an outlet for selling their art, whatever form it may take. In addition to fine paintings, drawings, and ceramics, one can find unique hand-knit sweaters and hand-painted greeting cards. Cape Fear Studios is located in the city center and is a great place to spend a Saturday afternoon in Fayetteville, browsing, admiring—and buying.

MUSEUM OF THE CAPE FEAR

One cannot speak of the arts in Fayetteville without mentioning another small and precious jewel. The Museum of the Cape Fear is a branch of the North Carolina Museum of History, but its exhibits are so artfully presented, so thoughtfully designed, as to make it a place the art-lover is drawn to. If one absorbs a bit of North Carolina history as well, so much the better!

FAYETTEVILLE SYMPHONY ORCHESTRA

For many, it is not the perfectly created painting or object that moves the spirit but the perfectly executed pas de deux or the singular solo of a virtuoso violinist. These art lovers, too, can find much in Fayetteville to make their spirits soar.

The Fayetteville Symphony Orchestra, the oldest community-supported cultural organization in

■ *Both visual and performing arts are appreciated in Fayetteville. On any given day, spirits may be lifted by the sweet sounds of the dulcimer in the Museum of the Cape Fear, by art displayed in the graphic arts studio of local artist Greg Hathaway, or perhaps by stirring music performed by the Fayetteville Symphony Orchestra.*

FROM POETRY AND POTTERY TO PHOTOGRAPHY AND PAINTING, THERE IS A GROUP OF FAYETTEVILLE RESIDENTS WORKING IN THE ART FORM.

Fayetteville, is an active group of about 60 volunteer musicians. Founded in 1957, the symphony is proud of its past and excited about what the future holds for the organization.

Conducted by Robert Gutter, who also conducts the Greensboro Symphony, the Fayetteville Symphony is overseen by a board of directors who are involved and enthusiastic. Lou Tippett, the president of the board, smilingly admits that she's not a musician herself, but she clearly believes the symphony is a valuable community asset that brings high-quality music to the residents of Fayetteville and the surrounding region.

The symphony brings two guest artists to the community every year, and in 1995, it agreed to co-produce a performance with the Cape Fear Regional Theater. Tippett says the orchestra is becoming increasingly professional in its approach to its annual program and looks forward to providing a valuable contribution to Fayetteville's cultural life in the years ahead.

OTHER MUSICAL TREATS

The North Carolina Symphony Orchestra appears several times each year in Fayetteville, always drawing an appreciative audience. And Fayetteville's Community Concert Series brings artists of the caliber of Tony Bennett, or the Mac Frampton Trio, to the city several times a year. The community concerts calendar is an eclectic one, providing treats for more than one musical taste.

Well-known musical performers also give concerts periodically at the Cumberland County Civic Center. Music enthusiasts of every persuasion, from fans of country to rock and roll to show tunes, are attracted to these concerts.

DANCE AND THEATER PERFORMANCES

Visiting artists who come to perform on the campuses of Fayetteville State University (FSU) and Methodist College are welcomed by the community at large. When the Alvin Ailey Repertory Ensemble comes to FSU—and it does—the audience is made up of modern dance fans from throughout the community.

If the purpose of art is to enlighten and inspire, to move the human spirit in a way that is memorable, then there is certainly a place in Fayetteville where that goal is achieved, night after night, year after year. The Cape Fear Regional Theater, which began as the Fayetteville Little Theater, is now staging world-class productions, from dramas to musicals to comedies.

Employing the dramatic skills of professional guest artists as well as the talents of some home-grown thespians, the theater achieves a higher level of professionalism in its productions than one might expect so far from the lights of Broadway.

Bo Thorp, the theater's artistic director, is an accomplished actress and director. 'She, and those who have worked with her, have created something extraordinary with the Cape Fear Regional Theater. Like so many who came to Fayetteville with a military spouse, she came, contributed what was uniquely hers, fell in love with Fayetteville, and, upon her husband's reentry to the civilian world, decided to stay and bring up a family. What a lucky place Fayetteville is to have drawn extraordinary people together who were eager and able to create such a dynamic community.

© Steven Aldridge

■ Well-known entertainers such as Tony Bennett (**left**) and the Oak Ridge Boys (**above right**) perform at the Cumberland County Civic Center. World-class productions are staged at the Cape Fear Regional Theater, under artistic director Bo Thorp (**above left**). Dr. Menno Pennink (**top**) makes his own music in the conservatory at his home.

A MULTITUDE OF
NEIGHBORHOODS

■ *Every home in Fayetteville comes alive with
color in the spring.*

■ *One of many apartment*
complexes in Fayetteville.

One of the reasons Fayetteville is such a special place is the diversity of its people, which is reflected in the wide range of neighborhoods in which the city's fascinating people live.

From the commanders of Fort Bragg and Pope AFB, who are required for professional reasons to live in designated quarters on post or on base, to new graduates in their first apartments of their own, to first-time home buyers, people in Fayetteville live in a variety of neighborhoods. Many of these areas are convenient to schools, shopping, and the city's employment centers. Many are also picturesque and striking architecturally. Some of Fayetteville's neighborhoods have defining characteristics. One upscale community, Greystone Farms, has all the amenities required by equestrians and horse owners; another, Kings Grant, touts a prize-winning golf course.

In spring and fall, however, some of the most ordinary subdivisions become spectacular as they are transformed by budding azaleas and dogwoods or by the golden hues of falling leaves.

More than 600 distinct neighborhoods dot the greater Fayetteville area. Some are within the city limits; others are in the farthest reaches of the surrounding countryside. They include large, new apartment complexes, complete with tennis courts and swimming pools, as well as older, more established communities with sidewalks and tree-lined streets. With a strong demand for housing suitable for young families, new subdivisions with ranch-style houses, carports, and yards for children to play in seem to spring up almost overnight.

AFFORDABLE HOUSING THAT MEETS PERSONAL NEEDS

Harry Sherrill, a real estate professional who was the 1995 president of the Fayetteville Realtors Association, says, "There's a home here for everyone." Pointing out that the median home price in Fayetteville in 1995 was $84,000, well below the national average and lower than in other cities in North Carolina, Sherrill is convinced that home ownership is well within the reach of almost all of Fayetteville's residents. Not surprisingly, more than 60 percent of the residents of the greater Fayetteville area are homeowners.

The home one chooses is dictated by economics, certainly, and by such practical considerations as the proximity of schools and work, but personal style is also important. In Fayetteville, one can find the right house and the right neighborhood, whether one is looking for a two-story with a history and well-established landscaping or a brand new split-level in a neighborhood where everyone is young and just starting out.

Sometimes, one finds the right house and the right neighborhood but still feels something is missing. Consider the example of Dr. Menno Pennink, a Fayetteville resident who is originally from Holland. A serious music devotee, Dr. Pennink wanted a special place in which to play his violin and cello and to accommodate his grand piano. He and his wife made their home uniquely suited to their personal needs by designing an addition that included a conservatory to the home they share with their children. Included in the addition were a swimming pool, a pool house, and the spacious conservatory in which Dr. Pennink can play his instruments

■ *Homes in Fayetteville satisfy the most discerning tastes, whether one wants a place to breed and race Rocky Mountain horses or a home like that of Dr. and Mrs. Menno Pennink, which includes a music conservatory.*

at any hour without disturbing the rest of the household. Adapting a house to become a family's perfect home is commonplace in Fayetteville, as evidenced by the many construction and home improvement companies thriving in the area.

Housing for Discerning Tastes

For professionals, like Dr. Pennink, and top-level executives with business and industry in Fayetteville, several neighborhoods offer upscale homes, with all the amenities that even the most discerning executive could expect. Van Story Hills is one of the longer-established neighborhoods with a high population of professionals, but there are others, in almost every quarter of the community. Woodbridge, in the northern section of Fayetteville, located across the street from Pine Forest High School, features large and lovely houses that are characerized as "executive homes" in real estate ads. Rayconda is another executive enclave, in a somewhat rural set-

ting. Kingsford and Woodlands are two relatively new areas, both within the city limits; each has spacious homes that feature all the latest in residential accoutrements.

Many neighborhoods in Fayetteville have lovely homes priced at less than $200,000 that could accommodate the executive who has arrived, as well as the professional who is still on the way up. The same can be said for the middle-level manager whose limit on the price of a house might be less than $100,000; the right house can be found in any number of neighborhoods, in any quarter of the city.

Tomorrow's Housing Market

Sherrill has some interesting predictions concerning Fayetteville's housing market as we approach the turn of the century.

"I think we'll see more townhouses being built," he says, "more golf communities, with smaller homes of 1,400—or 1,500—square feet or so being built around the golf course."

HERITAGE PLACE:
A Special Neighborhood

Heritage Place is a six-story building that is a neighborhood unto itself. A retirement community, Heritage Place is home to many of Fayetteville's older residents. The building, located on Cool Spring Street, is nestled in almost six acres of beautiful hardwood trees very near Cross Creek.

At a stage in life when a house and yard may be more work than they can manage, the residents of Heritage Place enjoy the amenities of any fine apartment building, as well as special touches designed especially for seniors, such as assist bars and an emergency call system in the bath areas and wide entrances and corridors.

Although even the smallest studio apartment has its own kitchenette, most residents prefer to gather for meals in the beautifully appointed dining room. A small library, roof terrace, and laundry facilities are also available. Trips to the beach, theater outings, shopping excursions, and visits to local restaurants provide a full schedule of events, supplemented by occasional in-house entertainment.

The monthly rental fees, which vary according to the size of the apartment and the number of residents, include transportation to doctors' offices and other places to transact business and shop. And there is no investment required to acquire one of Heritage Place's apartments.

Plans to add an assisted and skilled nursing care facility are in the works, which will make Heritage Place an even more attractive option for people of retirement age. Residents will be able to remain among familiar surroundings and friends, even if illness or injury should dictate an increased level of care.

Anne Gillon, who has been a resident of Heritage Place since it opened in 1983, is very happy with her home. She feels comfortable and secure.

"I am surrounded by caring people," she says, "and free from the worries and concerns I would face if I were living on my own."

■ *People in Fayetteville live in a variety of lovely communities. Wildflowers are in abundance at the Kings Grant golf community, while the senior officers' quarters at Fort Bragg are known for their Spanish mission-style architecture.*

■ *Beautiful homes, inside and out, are a hallmark of Fayetteville's neighborhoods. Members of the Fayetteville Garden Club are devoted to the aesthetic enhancement that plants and flowers can contribute to the home.*

His reasoning makes sense. As Sherrill points out, with the completion later this decade of the new Womack Army Medical Center at Fort Bragg, Fayetteville will become even more desirable as a retirement location, especially for people in the military. These retirees, many of whom are empty-nesters, will be looking for smaller homes, located relatively near the military installations and proximate to recreational opportunities.

There's an old saying among Army families, "Home is where the Army sends us," and that phrase, cross-stitched and framed, is hanging on many a wall in Fayetteville. The sentiment is a reality in the Air Force as well, and, as mobile a society as America has become, it could just as easily apply to executives with Monsanto, Kelly Springfield, or any number of other companies.

Housing for Retirees

There's no question that many people come to Fayetteville for a temporary stay. Whether it's a career move with DuPont, or military orders to Fort Bragg, many of Fayetteville's residents are transient. But many of these people choose to stay in Fayetteville when they have completed their careers or fulfilled their military obligations. Many choose to retire in Fayetteville. These people, be they a retired general manager of a large department store or a soldier who once commanded thousands of troops, are living throughout Fayetteville. They may retire next door to a young couple just beginning their lives together, or next door to the high school principal who taught their children. Or maybe they're moving into the golf community, where they'll spend all their time on the links!

MORE THAN 600 DISTINCT NEIGHBORHOODS DOT THE GREATER FAYETTEVILLE AREA, OFFERING AMENITIES FOR THE EQUESTRIAN, THE GOLFER, AND THE GARDENER.

A COMMUNITY FOR LIFELONG LEARNING

■ *A fresco painted by students on a wall near E. E. Smith High School, one of eight public high schools in Fayetteville, traces the history of African-Americans from slavery to modern times.*

ometimes Fayetteville's military identity eclipses the fact that it is also a college town. The city is home to Methodist College, a private four-year college, Fayetteville State University, a part of the University of North Carolina system, and Fayetteville Technical Community College, which offers two-year associate degree programs, as well as certificates and diplomas in selected fields.

Add to these schools the colleges and universities in close proximity to Fayetteville, such as Campbell University, in nearby Buies Creek, or Pembroke State University, in neighboring Robeson County, or those offering extension classes, such as Embry Riddle Aeronautical University or Central Michigan University, on the military installations, and one soon sees that there are abundant opportunities in the Fayetteville area to enhance one's postsecondary education.

COLLEGES AND UNIVERSITIES

Methodist College is one of the fastest-growing private colleges in the state. Located in the northern quadrant of Fayetteville, the campus is a local landmark, often visited by people attending concerts or other events at Reeves Auditorium, an acoustically perfect facility at the college. Based on an ambitious long-range plan for continued growth, enrollment could well be 2,200 students by the end of the decade, of whom 900 will be housed on campus.

Fayetteville State University is a constituent institution of the University of North Carolina system. Proud of its recent achievements in student enrollment and academic excellence, FSU offers 36 undergraduate degree programs and 16 graduate programs, including a doctoral degree in educational leadership.

Fayetteville Technical Community College (FTCC) provides an opportunity for students to earn an associate's degree in two years while earning college credits in such diverse programs as health services, business, and technical and vocational studies. Tuition is affordable, and financial assistance is often available.

FTCC also offers hundreds of adult continuing education classes at convenient locations throughout the community. The college has made a great contribution to the well-prepared and well-trained labor pool in Fayetteville.

Specialized degrees are also available at Carolina Bible College and Manna Christian College, both of which offer degrees in biblical studies. The Fayetteville branch of Shaw University, a four-year institution, offers B.A. degrees in public administration, criminal justice, business management, accounting, and behavioral science.

■ *During a break from classes, students at Fayetteville Technical Community College can enjoy the school's beautiful rose garden.*

*Fayetteville's educational facilities are challenged by the city's growth. Edgewood Elementary School (**upper right**) houses students from third through fifth grade; story hours are popular at the headquarters of the Cumberland County Library (**lower right**). At Fayetteville Technical Community College, construction is under way on new classroom facilities, dwarfing a one-room schoolhouse preserved on the college's grounds.*

PUBLIC SCHOOLS

The school systems of the city of Fayetteville and of Cumberland County merged in 1985. A decade later, the system has 50,000 students, 70 schools, and 5,000 employees, and it faces many of the same challenges and opportunities confronting large public school systems across America. The system has recently shown sustained improvement in some standardized test scores and, in some instances, they were in the top among public school systems in the state.

The Cumberland County schools include classes from kindergarten through 12th grade and are administered by a superintendent who is chosen by the nine-member elected Board of Education. Teachers are certified by the North Carolina Department of Education.

The public school system is an important part of the Fayetteville community, and it gets its fair share of public scrutiny. Eager to elevate the system's rankings among other systems in the state and country, school leaders have implemented a variety of initiatives to enhance teaching and learning in the classroom. These initiatives are paying off, and when they do, the satisfaction is sweet indeed. In one recent effort, teachers who had demonstrated an ability to teach writing skills instructed their colleagues systemwide in how to teach writing. The result? Higher scores across the board on an annual statewide writing test.

Aligning the curriculum to ensure that what is tested is being taught, and that what is taught is being tested, is another effort the

■ *Friendships and cheering at local football games are a part of student life in Fayetteville.*

school system is pursuing in order to improve its standing among other systems in the state.

The business community, knowing that an excellent education builds a viable workforce and the characters of future employees, has become actively involved in the Cumberland County schools through the Partners in Education program, an initiative of the school system and the Fayetteville Chamber of Commerce. Engineers from the Monsanto Company, for example, established a partnership with Cape Fear High School and began to work, one-on-one, with math students.

First Union Bank, at the request of Barbara Burgess, a teacher at the C. Wayne Collier Elementary School, established a program that enabled schoolchildren to open real bank accounts at school. The bank personnel were fifth-graders, all of whom were trained by the bank to be tellers, customer service representatives, data entry operators, and bank directors. The program has been very successful, according to Kerri Hurley of First Union Bank, who oversees some of the program. It's too soon to know, she says, if any

future bankers have been recruited from among the fifth-graders.

Steady, significant growth in Fayetteville and its environs has strained the school system's facilities in recent years. Like school systems elsewhere in the country, Cumberland County school leaders are pondering a variety of approaches to funding the construction necessary to accommodate current and projected growth.

The Fayetteville Chamber of Commerce was instrumental in building community support for a $40 million bond issue that passed in 1992. The Chamber's support for future bond issues, or other creative ways to finance new construction for new schools, will be essential. The Chamber's abiding interest in educational progress in Fayetteville is rooted in the knowledge that an excellent school system is an important asset to any community that wants to grow and thrive economically.

A truly excellent education is the most important asset a community can bestow on its young people. In Fayetteville, a partnership exists among business, education, civic, and religious leaders to make an excellent education a reality.

PRIVATE SCHOOLS

There are also several private schools in Fayetteville. The Fayetteville Academy, for example, offers classes from kindergarten through high school. Tuition is substantial, but the school is known to offer an excellent college preparatory curriculum. With fewer than 500 students and more than 50 instructors, the student/teacher ratio is enviable.

Among the church-affiliated schools offering enrollment in kindergarten through 12th grade are Cornerstone Christian Academy, affiliated with Cornerstone Baptist Church; Fayetteville Christian School, which emphasizes its interdenominational Christian environment; Berean Baptist Academy; Trinity Christian School; and College Lakes Christian Academy.

Northwood Temple Academy, affiliated with Northwood Temple Church, and the parochial schools affiliated with St. Ann's Church and St. Patrick's Church offer classes from kindergarten through eighth grade.

Other private schools include the Haynie School, which was established in 1938, and the Guy School. Both accept students through the fourth grade.

The Montessori School of Fayetteville offers a preprimary program for children ages three through six. Many of the church-affiliated schools also offer preschool enrollment for children of three and four.

Becoming educated is, to a great degree, a matter of personal motivation. Any child, and any adult, who has the desire to learn can become educated in Fayetteville.

■ *St. Ann's Church (lower right) offers classes from kindergarten through eighth grade. Outside the classroom, many businesses and cultural organizations offer programs for schoolchildren. At lower left, a docent begins a tour of the art museum.*

MANY FAITHS IN FAYETTEVILLE

■ *The annual Gathering of the Clans at Highland Presbyterian Church is a stirring ritual. For others, the meditation garden at St. John's Episcopal Church (**below**) is an oasis of calm.*

*F*aith in God has been strong among Fayettevillians since the city's founding, when the Scottish settlers brought with them the tenets of Presbyterianism.

Today, Fayetteville has many established churches as well as mosques and a synagogue, and there is a local Society of Friends, or Quakers. Though the religious beliefs may vary from denomination to denomination, even from one congregation to another, living a righteous life is a precept Fayettevillians of many religious faiths follow. Whatever one's faith, one can find souls of similar persuasion in Fayetteville. In the tradition of southern hospitality, the area's houses of worship stand ready to welcome newcomers as well as long-time residents.

Southern Baptist and Free Will Baptist congregations are represented by more than 100 churches in the weekly listing of churches published each Saturday in the *Fayetteville Observer-Times*. Methodists run a close second.

As one might expect, some of the most memorable services in Fayetteville take place during the Christmas and Easter seasons. Snyder Memorial Baptist Church presents an annual program called the Singing Christmas Tree, which is often standing room only. The "tree" is made up of singers from the church's choir, and their renditions of traditional Christmas songs are poignantly beautiful.

First Presbyterian Church, which will celebrate its bicentennial anniversary in the year 2000, is architecturally one of the most beautiful churches in Fayetteville. At Easter, it seems even more so, as the springtime blossoms decorate its grounds.

In coming together and attempting to address the ills of this world as they prepare for the next, churchgoers in Fayetteville are neither a solemn nor a sanctimonious lot. One can

hear many a joyful noise being made to the Lord on Sunday mornings when the choirs of the city's churches lift their voices.

CHURCHES OF BEAUTY AND HISTORY

Many of Fayetteville's churches are beautiful structures, and some have long and fascinating histories. St. John's Episcopal Church on Green Street, for example, was established in 1816. It was the site of General William Westmoreland's wedding in 1947 to Katherine S. ("Kitty") Van Deusen, the daughter of a career military officer who retired to Fayetteville. The church features lovely stained-glass windows that were made in Munich, Germany, and installed in 1899. Authentic Tiffany stained-glass windows are also a striking feature of St. Joseph's Episcopal Church, on Moore Street.

A CULTURE OF CARING

Of course, it's much more than buildings that make a church. The unity of the people who make up the congregation, and the work they do in this world, is what makes a church a living entity. The good works being done by churches in Fayetteville are incalculable. They include acts of generosity, kindness, and caring carried out so quietly that they often go unnoticed by the media and the masses.

One place where good works are certainly being carried out is at Highland Presbyterian Church. The pastor, Ernest Johnson, has become involved in community initiatives to such an extent that he was named one of four outstanding Chamber of Commerce members in 1994. He earned this distinction by serving as chair of MetroVisions, a Chamber committee charged with forging a vision for Fayetteville's future. Ernest Johnson is also active in a community

■ *The annual Singing Christmas Tree program at the Snyder Memorial Baptist Church is a truly uplifting experience.*

group known as Bridges, Inc., which provides help to poverty-stricken families with children, but this is help that is distinctly different from charity. The group offers help in dealing with educational challenges, in maintaining family cohesiveness, in learning how to be an effective parent, and in providing constructive playtime activities for children with few options. Johnson's congregation is firmly behind him in his civic and humanitarian efforts.

C. R. Edwards, pastor emeritus of First Baptist Church, has extended the instinct to look after his pastoral flock into the political arena. He is a state senator, representing his Fayetteville constituency with dignity and honor in the general assembly in Raleigh.

The churches of Fayetteville are an important partner in many other initiatives intended to address community needs. Fayetteville Urban Ministry, an interdenominational organization, receives a portion of its funding from area churches. That support, along with other funding, makes possible some of the most far-reaching community programs in Fayetteville.

One of the most important of the Urban Ministry's efforts is an adult literacy program, which has taught hundreds of adults to read; its enviable success rate is 90 percent. The Urban Ministry also provides cut wood to low-income families to heat their homes, as well as financial assistance in paying fuel or utility bills.

Find-a-Friend, another program of the Urban Ministry, matches caring adults with troubled youngsters in an effort to provide one-on-one mentoring and assistance in getting and staying on the right path in life.

Yet another Urban Ministry initiative is the Nehemiah Project, which provides help in maintaining and renovating the homes of low-income fami-

lies in Fayetteville. A new roof or storm windows can be helpful in reducing future heating costs, so the cost of providing this assistance is seen as an investment that continues to benefit the recipient well into the future.

Another caring organization in Fayetteville is the CARE Clinic, which offers free primary medical and dental care to low-income, uninsured families in the city. Started by a group of volunteer physicians in 1993, who saw how great the need was and how overburdened the social services programs had become, the CARE Clinic is totally staffed by volunteers. Physicians, nurses, other health-care professionals, and even the secretary and maintenance staff are volunteers. The clinic is sustained by the extraordinary commitment of these volunteers and private financial contributions.

Habitat for Humanity in Fayetteville proudly claims hundreds of volunteers who build houses for low-income families. The beneficiaries of the program, the potential homeowners, contribute their own "sweat equity" in constructing the houses and often become volunteers who help build houses for others.

These are but a few of the programs under way in Fayetteville that are making it a better place for all its residents. Almost every church has a program that is intended to encourage children and young people to be involved in wholesome activity that will help them develop into responsible, productive adults. Bible schools, summer camps, after-school activities, and other such programs are all available in Fayetteville to help its children.

Fayetteville is a city on the move, confident and cosmopolitan, with great aspirations for its economic future. But it remains a city with a heart, a heart big enough to care for all its people.

■ *Although Fayetteville is a city on the move, Fayettevillians still respect long-held traditions, such as observing the Jewish sabbath, handing down bibles from generation to generation, and, as a statue of St. Francis reminds them, to be generous quietly.*

HAVING FUN IN FAYETTEVILLE

■ *For youngsters, nothing beats a trip to the circus, while their parents might relish a few moments of quiet at a concert in the park.*

un means different things to different people, in Fayetteville as elsewhere. For some in Fayetteville, it's a long afternoon on a well-manicured golf course; for others, it's a night on the town, doing the latest dance steps to the latest tunes; for still others who are young and energetic, it's skateboarding at the Skatepark.

RECREATIONAL OPPORTUNITIES

In Fayetteville, recreational opportunities abound. The City of Fayetteville Parks and Recreation Department oversees 39 athletic facilities and recreational areas, including basketball courts, some of which are illuminated, six tennis courts, a swimming pool, numerous baseball and softball fields, and Skatepark. The department also administers 10 recreation centers throughout the city, one for senior citizens and one for citizens who have special recreational needs because of mental or physical handicaps.

Mazarick Park, located just off Bragg Boulevard, one of Fayetteville's busiest thoroughfares, is an 80-acre oasis of picnic shelters, fishing areas, playgrounds, tennis courts, and nature trails. Clark Park, just off Ramsey Street, another busy byway, is somewhat more geared to the nature enthusiast. The park's nature center offers displays of North Carolina's wildlife and botanical specimens.

The Fayetteville Parks and Recreation Department also has a delightful museum within its purview. Fascinate-U Children's Museum, aptly named, offers hands-on learning experiences that enthrall children. With admission just $1.00, many parents have found it to be the best entertainment bargain around.

For outdoor fun outside the city limits, there is Arnette Park, a 100-acre park owned and maintained by Cumberland County, near North Carolina Highway 87. The park includes picnic shelters, lighted baseball and softball fields, horseshoe pits, and a sand volleyball court.

For some, an evening at the ballpark

is the best way to have summertime fun. The Fayetteville Generals, a farm team of the Detroit Tigers, play a full-season schedule of games at the J. P. Riddle Stadium on Legion Road. The stadium is named for the late Fayettevillian who developed many of the city's neighborhoods, shopping areas, and commercial districts and who donated the land on which the stadium stands.

Soccer enthusiasts in Fayetteville are delighted with the fast pace with which the Fayetteville Area Soccer Complex became a reality. Located on the grounds of Methodist College, the complex features eight soccer fields and a practice field, as well as paved parking and a clubhouse.

Rivaling similar facilities in Charlotte and Greensboro, the Fayetteville complex is a result of generous local private support. Dr. and Mrs. Bill Jordan contributed $400,000, which was quickly matched by other donations.

The fields are expected to draw thousands of visitors to Fayetteville for regional soccer tournaments.

FESTIVALS, FESTIVALS, FESTIVALS

Fayettevillians love their festivals, whatever the occasion. In celebration of blooming dogwoods, blazing azaleas, and other springtime delights, the Dogwood Festival brings many Fayettevillians out from year to year for a variety of activities, including barbecue cook-offs, street dances, and concerts.

The Dogwood Festival has grown from its inception in the early 1980s to become Fayetteville's premier festival. Timed to take place when the dogwoods and azaleas bloom, the spring festival culminates with Sunday on the Square, an Arts Council-sponsored event that brings thousands of people to the center of Fayetteville for an afternoon-long celebration of music, food, arts, crafts, performances—in a word, fun!

■ *Fayettevillians enjoy many outdoor activities. At Clark Park, park ranger Tammy Calvin can introduce them to a corn snake. And when the dogwoods and azaleas are glorious, in spring, they can watch the parade during the Dogwood Festival.*

The International Folk Festival, which takes place in early autumn, also brings thousands to the city center, where they can enjoy the authentic foods, music, colorful costumes, and cultural displays of many nations.

The Hellenic Festival is another popular annual event. Sponsored by the Greek community of Fayetteville, the event is well attended by members of the local community, especially those who are eager to eat authentic Greek food and to enjoy bouzouki music and spirited dancing.

Fayetteville is located very near Spivey's Corner, so attending the annual Hollerin' Contest, which put that little town on the map, is a fun way to spend a Saturday in June. If you're talented at summoning swine, you could be a winner in the crowded field of competitors!

FAYETTEVILLE AFTER DARK

The night life in Fayetteville, not surprisingly, given the city's demographics, is geared to the young and the energetic. On any given weekend night, the dance floors across town are packed. Some nightspots draw the boot-scootin' duos; the Electric Sliders are doing their thing at any number of places across town; and beach music aficionados are at Flaherty's, doing that perennial southern favorite, the shag. Even alternative music lovers have a favorite haunt; if there's moshing going on in Fayetteville, it will be at Neo's, which unabashedly advertises its "grunge" atmosphere.

More sedate party animals may well be at the Highland Country Club or a dance at the VFW. But the fact remains that night life in Fayetteville is lived to the fullest primarily by those people who spend their daytime hours in college classes or who leap from airplanes as part of a day's work.

One area of Fayetteville that reflects the youthful character of the community is the stretch of McPherson Church Road that has come to be known as Restaurant Row. From the Outback Steakhouse, to Bennigan's, to Hooters, and at a score of other restaurants, parking lots are filled on every weekend night. The food is good at whichever

restaurant one chooses, and the music is mostly contemporary and just a tad too loud for someone of middle age. High spirits are evident, and it is here that one sees the youthful exuberance of a population that is largely under 30.

There's enough going on in Fayetteville to fill the calendar of even the most social of butterflies. Whether it's a dinner out with friends, or hitting the dance floor, or catching a concert by a legendary talent like B. B. King at the Cumberland County Civic Center, there's much to do in Fayetteville after dark. Several movie theaters show the latest Hollywood releases; or you can rent your all-time favorite movie at any of the many video rental stores in town. For those who want more active entertainment, there's always the skating rinks, including Fort Bragg's ice rink, which is open to the public. For some, there is nothing more fun than watching someone else try to ice skate for the first time.

People in Fayetteville love to entertain, and they do so by blending the camaraderie of new friends, old

wine, and good food, and often by bringing together disparate people of diverse backgrounds. Their hospitality may take the form of a cookout on the patio or an elegant and formal dinner party. But, whatever the occasion, southern hospitality abounds.

Some of Fayetteville's neighborhoods have become so congenial that the residents come together twice a year. These "neighbors only" events often include a pig-pickin' during the summer and a more formal dinner during the winter holiday season.

Fayetteville is an exciting place to live, too. There's no thrill quite like seeing hundreds of airborne troopers parachuting to earth, returning safely after a deployment that has kept them and Fayetteville in the forefront of international news. New Orleans may have the French Quarter and Memphis may have Beale Street, but they don't have the crème de la crème of America's fighting forces at Fort Bragg and Pope Air Force Base. Just as the tourist ad for the city says, "Fayetteville is used to having large crowds 'drop in' all the time." And there's no party quite like that.

THE CULTURE OF COMMERCE

Five-year-old Amber plays Putt-Putt® golf, which originated in Fayetteville 40 years ago.

ayetteville is a great city in which to do business.

There are many reasons this is true: the city's growing market, the stable economic base of a large military payroll, the convenient location, and the entrepreneurial spirit, which leads to the creation of new, innovative businesses.

Fayetteville is a city in which it can be said, and often is, "Business is good!" When challenging economic downturns do occur, optimism and the long view usually prevail. Such downturns can be suddenly invoked in Fayetteville by incidents in far-away places, requiring the deployment of significant numbers of troops from Fort Bragg and Pope Air Force Base. During the Persian Gulf War, for example, Fayetteville suffered through a prolonged deployment, but the city rebounded when the troops returned.

The direct and indirect economic impact of the military on Fayetteville's trade area economy is about $4 billion annually. But there is more than just camouflage green in the local economy, and those who contribute to Fayetteville's healthy economy in other ways have a valuable role to play in the city's future.

All of America has come to enjoy a recreational activity whose business roots are in Fayetteville. In 1954, Don Clayton was feeling the effects of a stressful career as an insurance executive. Ordered by doctors to rest for a full 30 days, Clayton instead spent his time developing the concept of Putt-Putt® golf. Forty years later, miniature golf courses can be found worldwide, and they have evolved into true family entertainment centers, incorporating the latest video technology while enabling young and old alike to enjoy the pure and simple fun of putting. The country's first Putt-Putt course is on Fayetteville's Bragg Boulevard.

■ *Fayettevillians and visitors attend concerts, conventions, and other events at the Cumberland County Civic Center.*

There's no relationship quite like that among colleagues.

In Fayetteville, several organizations cultivate this relationship by bringing people together who are engaged in the same kind of work. Associations for realtors, insurance professionals, legal secretaries, and others maintain active memberships. There are five local chapters of the American Business Women's Association, a national organization, as well as a Business and Professional Women's Club. Many of these groups are active in civic affairs as well as in furthering the professional standing of their members. Some provide scholarships so that deserving local students can acquire the education necessary to enter the profession.

Another local group, Networth, is made up of about 100 women who are engaged in a profession or who own or manage a business. Celebrating its 15th anniversary in 1995, the group has a long-held tradition of awarding annual scholarships to young women who aspire to become students at Fayetteville State University, Fayetteville Technical Community College, or Methodist College with an end goal of entering the business or professional world.

Each year, Networth awards $4,500 in scholarships to as many as six young women.

Though the workplace has changed for women in the 15 years of Networth's existence, and more and more opportunities have come available for women to succeed in the business world, professional women still need to come together and share the experiences they enjoy—and those they don't. Networth's primary raison d'être is to help each member network in the local business community. Among the members are current and former elected officials, bankers, doctors, attorneys, educators, entrepreneurs, and managers.

Suzanne Pennink, owner of Suzanne Barlow Realtors, is one such member. She values the interaction with other professional women.

"Networth has allowed me to meet women who have experience in specific fields," she says. "If I have a question about local schools, or banking, or cellular phones, in Networth there's a woman to whom I can go with a question. Men have always had their associations. I think Networth was formed to offer the same kind of networking opportunity to professional women."

North Carolina Natural Gas Corporation, a local distribution company with 22 other locations in the eastern and south-central sections of the state, is another successful business that got its start in Fayetteville. So is Mid-South Insurance Company, a firm known for insuring small employers for employee benefits, primarily health insurance.

Although not every business begun in Fayetteville goes on to become a nationally known enterprise, every business in Fayetteville has access to the advice, guidance, informational resources, and encouragement that helped long-lived companies survive and flourish. The Fayetteville Chamber of Commerce provides much support for new and small businesses. So, too, does the Small Business Technology and Development Center (SBTDC), which is a business and technology extension service that operates as an interinstitutional program of the University of North Carolina. Working closely with the Small Business Administration, SBTDC centers throughout the state of North Carolina stand ready to help aspiring entrepreneurs get started and, more important perhaps, survive the rough initial startup phase of a new business.

Fayetteville's healthy regard for those who engage in business and commerce is well founded. Business provides an opportunity for those with talent and a willingness to work to rise to the top of their fields; it is businesspeople who understand the necessity of adapting and adjusting, embracing new ideas as a way of improving products and services; it is business that serves as one of America's most beloved ambassadors, by virtue of its prod-

ucts and services, which are recognized around the world; and business is an eager learner, whose research and development efforts have resulted in discoveries that enhance the lives of all Americans.

In Fayetteville, business and commerce are celebrated annually with ChamberFest, a series of events sponsored by the Chamber of Commerce. From seminars to soigné social events, from golf and tennis competitions to the casual and much-anticipated Oyster Roast, ChamberFest brings business professionals together to celebrate the honorable pursuit of business in which they are all engaged.

The Chamber of Commerce has many allies that contribute to Fayetteville's supportive climate for business. The Fayetteville Area Economic Development Corporation, in addition to recruiting new industry to the Fayetteville area, places business expansion and retention among its goals. Each May, the FAEDC sponsors Industry Appreciation Month, which focuses the entire community's attention on the importance of existing industry and business to Fayetteville's economic health. These efforts preclude Fayetteville from becoming complacent about the abundance and diversity of businesses that have chosen to locate here; as a community, Fayetteville does not take the continued presence of these businesses for granted.

The Fayetteville Area Economic Development Corporation and the Chamber of Commerce work as partners in nurturing and developing the economic climate in Fayetteville. In the view of many, if Fayetteville is a community to be "sold" to prospective new industry, then it is the Chamber that is heading up product development, through its efforts to improve the overall quality of life as it works to improve the profitability of its members.

In recent years, local government has done much to reinforce the Chamber's commitment to providing an inviting arena for business and industry. For example, the Fayetteville Area Economic Development Corporation recently convinced Cumberland County commissioners to create the Industrial Development Contingency Fund.

While requiring no new taxes, this innovative approach calls for the county to set aside 50 percent of any new tax revenues gained when an industry with more than a $1 million investment locates to Fayetteville or an existing industry undergoes the equivalent expansion. The revenue that is set aside will be used for a variety of incentives to attract still more new industry. This is an enlightened approach to eco-

nomic development and a strong signal that local government comprehends the need for a strong business and industrial component to the community.

THE OLDE FAYETTEVILLE ASSOCIATION

Fayetteville, like innumerable other cities across America, has faced the phenomenon of urban flight, the movement of businesses—and people—away from the center of the city. As population centers began to develop away from Fayetteville's uptown, once the setting for all shopping and business, the inexorable departure of businesses began.

The Olde Fayetteville Association, an organization existing to breathe economic and civic life into the center of the city, has enjoyed a significant measure of success. As a sponsor of events in the city center, the association has succeeded in attracting crowds of people for festivals and

■ *Eliza Currie inspects between 400 and 500 tires a day at Kelly-Springfield Tire Company, one of Fayettteville's largest employers.*

other fun special occasions that have taken place on the cobbled and tree-lined streets in the area.

The Olde Fayetteville Association has also been an important partner with the FAEDC and other community agencies in recruiting new business to Fayetteville's city center. From a business point of view, there is much to commend this part of town as a potential location. There are many unique, historically significant, large buildings to house a business. And, although prices could escalate rapidly if a new redevelopment initiative is successful, downtown property is currently relatively inexpensive. In 1993, Somar, a telemarketing company, established an

office in Fayetteville, taking advantage of a former bank building, in good condition and with ample parking, to locate its telemarketers.

Like the FAEDC, the Olde Fayetteville Association includes retention in its mission, and it takes care to keep city center businesses informed of what is happening. A quarterly newsletter, the *Downtown Turnaround*, is sent to 2,500 business and civic leaders throughout Fayetteville, reinforcing the idea that the city center is a good place to do business and that its reincarnation as an energetic place for professional, cultural, and business activity will benefit the entire Fayetteville community.

A Retail Magnet

Fayetteville is the city of choice for shopping not only for its residents but for those in a surrounding 10-county area. Fayetteville's reputation as a retail mecca is well founded in its abundance and variety of shopping opportunities. The North Carolina Department of Revenue has deemed the Cross Creek Mall intersection the busiest shopping area in the state, based on dollars per square foot. This busy hub includes not only Cross Creek Mall itself, with its 100-plus stores and eateries, but several other nearby shopping centers, all within a two-square-mile area: Cross Creek Plaza, with Walmart, as well as Office Depot and other stores; Cross Pointe Centre, with T. J. Maxx and Discovery Zone among its premier tenants; Westwood Shopping Center, with a Rose's, Talbots, and the Pilgrim, a delightful locally owned specialty store; McPherson Square, with the Strawberry Barn, an upscale ladies' clothing store; and MarketFair Mall, with several clothing and shoe stores.

Other fine shopping centers are easily reached from the Cross Creek intersection. The attractive and convenient Bordeaux Shopping Center, Tallywood Shopping Center, and Eutaw Shopping Center include branch locations of larger department and discount stores, as well as one-of-a-kind shops where one can find Fayetteville's best selection of newspapers or periodicals, personalized gift items, and the most shopper-friendly delicatessen in which to stop for a mid-shopping spree snack.

Retail giants represented in Fayetteville include Walmart, which has three busy stores in the Fayetteville area; Sam's Club, a volume outlet store, affiliated with Walmart; J. C. Penney's and Sears department stores; grocery stores, including Harris Teeter, Food Lion, and Kroger; drug stores, such as Revco, Phar-Mor, and Eckerd Drugs; building supply stores, such as Lowe's and Home Depot; auto supply outlets, such as Pep Boys, Advance Auto Parts, and Western Auto; and clothing stores ranging from the discount chain T. J. Maxx to Lerner Shops to the Limited to Talbots.

The result of all this shopping activity is annual retail sales in Cumberland County exceeding $2 billion, a number that increases every year.

Manufacturing and Distribution

Not all the business being done in Fayetteville is conducted in shops and malls; there's a substantial manufacturing presence, including such industrial giants as Monsanto, Kelly-Springfield Tire Company, Black & Decker, and DuPont.

Kelly-Springfield Tire Company, which employs about 3,000 people, is one of Fayetteville's largest employers. Its huge plant, on Fayetteville's northern outskirts, is the largest tire-manufacturing plant under one roof in the world. The plant operates 24 hours a day, and at shift-change times, it's easy to see from the heavy traffic around the plant that Kelly-Springfield plays a large role in the lives of many Fayettevillians.

More than 12,000 jobs are affiliated with manufacturing in the Fayetteville area. From the teams of workers assembling fans and small heaters at Fasco's recently modernized manufacturing plant to the chemical engineers at the Monsanto's plant, which recently initiated a $25 million expansion,

One of the retail businesses that many people in Fayetteville are happy to know about is Rhudy's Jewelry Showroom. In fact, once a relationship is established with Rhudy's, it is usually a long and mutually satisfactory one.

Rhudy Phillips is the owner of the company, which features one of the most breathtaking displays of gold and other jewelry this side of a Middle Eastern souk. On a typical Saturday, the level of activity in the shop can approach that of a busy bazaar, with customers shopping, browsing, bringing in this piece or that for repair, or stopping by for a consultation on just what the right gift would be for a particular occasion.

Through it all, Rhudy Phillips presides, aided by the most courteous and knowledgeable sales-people one will encounter anywhere. The selection of merchandise is almost overwhelming, and the prices are reasonable. But one of the most enduring assets Rhudy's has going for it is its well-earned reputation for honesty and extraordinary customer service.

One southern executive, who once lived in Fayetteville, has continued to do all his jewelry business with Rhudy, from locations as far afield as Washington, D.C., and Atlanta. He thinks nothing of leaving a Rolex watch with Rhudy's trusted associate, Joe Brunais, knowing it will be returned to him with the necessary work properly completed.

Rhudy's Jewelry Showroom is a member of the Fayetteville Chamber of Commerce, and Rhudy himself is an advocate for the Chamber's initiatives to strengthen the ties between the military and civilian population. A Korean War-era veteran, Rhudy displays the official photos of many high-ranking military officers in his shop, most of them personally inscribed with best wishes.

Recently, Rhudy's expanded its inventory to include small furniture, decorative and gift items, and unique objects of art. A business that is uniquely Fayetteville's, Rhudy's is a part of the mosaic that is Fayetteville's retail community.

A Complete Fayetteville
Once & For All

The focus of the Olde Fayetteville Association is on the city center, and its aim is to see that part of the city become a place that draws people to it. The members of the association harbor no unrealistic expectations that the retail magnet of Fayetteville will revert to the city center. But they do believe it is possible to make this part of town a beautiful place, a unique place, for visitors and residents alike.

There are many people in Fayetteville who aspire to see the center of Fayetteville restored to its former vibrancy. Even those who rarely venture into Fayetteville's center would prefer to know that the heart of the city they love is a beautiful, functional place. Some of these people have invested a great deal of their own resources in recruiting businesses to this part of town. Most of these businesses cater primarily to the workers in the government offices in the vicinity. The Radisson Prince Charles Hotel is owned by a group of local investors; Hickory Hams & Deli, owned by Fayetteville native George Matthews, is located in the same building occupied by the United Way and the studios and offices of WZFX 99.1 ("The Fox").

In 1995, a delegation of 40 or so key representatives from various constituencies of the community came together in an initiative that has come to be known as "A Complete Fayetteville, Once and For All." Working with distinguished landscape architect Robert E. Marvin of South Carolina, who is the lead consultant for the undertaking, the group intends to transform the city center into a continually developing "heart" for the city.

Robert E. Marvin and his associates have an impressive track record in accomplishing just such transformations. Columbia, South Carolina, now has a beautiful park as its city center, replacing uninviting and unattractive rail yards. Beaufort, South Carolina, is another southern community that has benefited from the design expertise of Robert Marvin's firm. The company has received awards from four First Ladies as well as other national recognition.

88   *F*AYETTEVILLE

To establish a professional relationship with Marvin, Fayetteville raised an initial consulting fee of $450,000, which included $80,000 in private contributions, $232,000 from the city of Fayetteville, and $138,000 from Cumberland County. This initial fee is being divided among Marvin & Associates as lead consultants, HyettPalma, a Virginia-based marketing research company, and Smith Advertising & Associates, a Fayetteville public relations firm.

No one is expecting that $450,000 will transform Fayetteville's city center—from the beginning, Marvin and others associated with this initiative have estimated that it will almost certainly require a multimillion dollar commitment. But this initial consultation does buy the following:

- A review of the more than 26 "revitalization" plans that have been undertaken in past years and a combined, updated version to be considered for implementation.
- A series of information-gathering focus meetings with various se ments of the community to discern what the community wants in its city center.
- A proposed design, to be presented to the Action Committee overseeing the Fayetteville Once and for All initiative.
- Design documentation, in written and graphic form, to serve as the communication vehicle for the project.
- Support studies, intended to focus on issues that are identified in the preceding phases.
- Implementation. Marvin's design team will help the Action Committee, local government, developers, and other components of the city implement the master plan.

If "A Complete Fayetteville, Once and For All" is ultimately successful in re-creating Fayetteville's city center as an attractive, functional "heart" for Fayetteville, it will be one more reason Fayetteville will be an excellent city for business. Providing an inviting environment for the people who work in the city center, and for the people who would be inspired to visit this part of Fayetteville, this initiative is a noble effort to make Fayetteville all that it can be—once and for all.

Fayettevillians are making products and manufacturing goods that enhance the lives of people around the world. At a time when service-related industries comprise much of America's gross domestic product, it's noteworthy that manufacturing still plays an important role in Fayetteville's economy.

Another well-known manufacturer, Maidenform, Inc., is a relative newcomer to Fayetteville's family of businesses and industries. Maidenform built a large distribution center in Fayetteville in 1992, from which employees export, worldwide, about half a million inspected and tagged garments each week.

The hospitality and tourism industry emerged in the early 1990s as a strong component of Fayetteville's economy. More than 8,000 people in the city are employed in the tourism and hospitality industry, and in 1993 the total economic impact of travel-related expenditures amounted to $277 million.

HEALTH CARE 99

Fayetteville is striving to become the health-care center for the region, which will certainly enhance the city economically. The city aims to fill that role for the surrounding nine-county area by 1999, the same year the new, large, and technologically state-of-the-art Womack Army Medical Center at Fort Bragg is scheduled to open.

Health Care 99 (HC 99) is Fayetteville's initiative to establish the city as a regional medical center. The Fayetteville Chamber of Commerce has been in the forefront of this worthy project since it was undertaken in April 1993. It is appropriate that at the same time Fayetteville reaches its goal of serving as the region's health-care center, the Chamber of Commerce will be celebrating its centennial anniversary.

Excellent medical care is certainly available in Fayetteville. In addition to Womack Army Medical Center, which will serve the military population and

■ *Excellent medical care is available at such modern facilities as Highsmith-Rainey Memorial Hospital (**left**) or the public health center.*

■ *Fayettevillians are conscientious, productive workers, whether they are inspecting a roll of film at Qualex, Inc. (**top**), tagging and shipping garments at the distribution center of Maidenform, Inc. (**bottom**), or checking the presses that print the* Fayetteville Observer-Times.

retirees, Fayetteville is home to Cape Fear Valley Medical Center, a county-owned hospital that has experienced rapid growth and enhancement in recent years; Highsmith-Rainey Hospital, which is owned and operated by Columbia Hospital Corporation of America, is also an excellent hospital. Finally, the Veterans Affairs Hospital in Fayetteville serves 160,000 veterans in North and South Carolina. Plans for the future include a 120-bed nursing home-care unit and an expansion of the ambulatory care area. A sign at the entrance to the hospital bears the poignant message "The price of freedom is visible here," a sentiment that Fayetteville understands completely.

With the scrutiny being given to ways to reduce health-care costs, many in Fayetteville are looking for ways to reduce the amount of time a patient spends in the hospital. One of the most responsive health-care facilities in this regard is the Fayetteville Ambulatory Surgery Center. Patients may check in early in the day, undergo a surgical procedure, and, after a brief period of monitored recovery, be released to convalesce at home.

Physicians abound in Fayetteville, specializing in any number of areas of medicine. The health-care needs of a generally healthy family can be met easily in Fayetteville, but so can the more specific health-care needs of those who have a chronic medical condition.

The overarching goal of Health Care 99 is to enhance and build upon what is already available in the Fayetteville region, creating a coordinated, regional system of health care that will provide services in the areas of prevention, treatment, and

rehabilitation. The dedicated corps of volunteers who are at work to make this vision a reality are already achieving success in meeting their specific incremental goals.

Chaired initially by Gerald Strand, Ph.D., of the Fayetteville Area Health Education Center, who was succeeded by Stephen Smith of Interim HealthCare, HC 99 received a substantial grant early on from the Kate B. Reynolds Charitable Trust and elicited significant private sector funding. HC 99 has also received national and international recognition. In April 1995, just two years after being established, HC 99 was recognized by the HealthCare Forum of San Diego, California, for honorable mention in the category of small, rural, and regional health-care initiatives.

Health Care 99, as an affiliate of the Fayetteville Chamber, was recently appointed by North Carolina as the community sponsor of an 11-county health insurance purchasing alliance. This alliance is a tremendous boon for small businesses in the region and will make high-quality, low-cost insurance available to thousands of small businesses and their employees.

A STRONG ECONOMIC FUTURE
Fayetteville's economy and its strength as a retail center look promising as the city works proactively to bolster its industrial component and takes action to establish a new economic base with health care-related businesses. These activities, combined with the stable presence of the large military payroll, will insure that Fayetteville remains an excellent city in which to do business far into the twenty-first century.

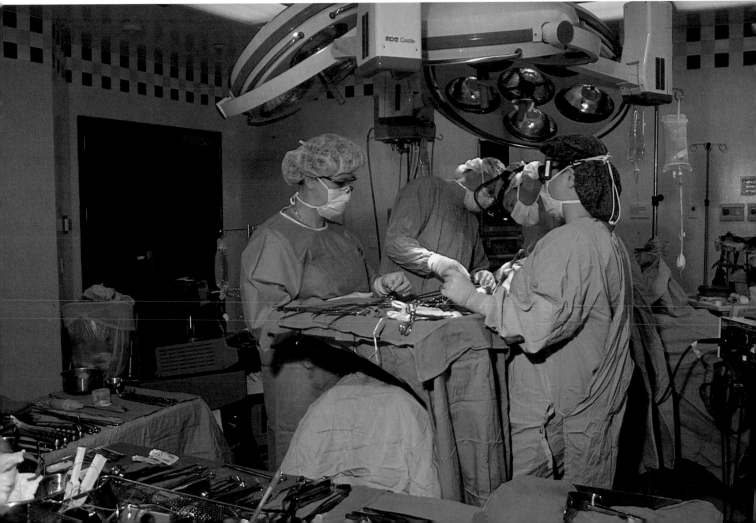

THE MILITARY CULTURE

■ *Iron Mike, symbol of the 82D Airborne trooper.*

*F*ort Bragg and Pope Air Force Base are two distinctly different installations, of two very different military services. Fort Bragg and Pope AFB also have very different missions, but though separate and distinct, their missions are inextricably linked in a world that presents new and different challenges to those charged with defending America's vital interests, wherever on the globe those interests are threatened. Together, Fort Bragg and Pope Air Force Base form one of the largest, most important military complexes in the world.

People in Fayetteville are proud Fort Bragg and Pope Air Force Base are next-door neighbors, and the influence of the military is infused throughout the greater community. The "whump, whump, whump" of helicopters flying in formation overhead, the scream of a high-flying military jet, the rhythmic cadence of a jody call as soldiers keep pace on an early-morning run—all these sounds are familiar to Fayettevillians.

By virtue of being one of the U.S. Army's largest posts and an open installation, with no gates to preclude passage onto or through it, Fort Bragg is perhaps Fayetteville's better-known military neighbor. Pope Air Force Base is, for security reasons, closed to general traffic, and one must check in through a security gate to gain access to the base. But the presence of both military installations, and the people who serve in the Army and the Air Force, are valued highly in Fayetteville. Further, the military presence provides an economic bedrock for the local economy.

With a combined total of almost 47,000 military personnel assigned to Fort Bragg and Pope AFB, the total military payroll in 1994 was well over $1 billion. Add to that the combined annual payroll of almost $170 million for the almost 12,000 civilian employees who work on the two installations, and it's easy to see why the military presence is of such economic significance in Fayetteville. When one considers other military expenditures, the money spent on local goods and services, the total economic impact of Fort Bragg and Pope Air Force Base is in the billions of dollars.

The interest Fayetteville has in maintaining the presence of its military neighbors is far more than mercenary, however. Fayetteville has in recent years enthusiastically embraced the designation of military town. Proud of Fort Bragg? You bet! Pleased to be the home of Pope Air Force Base? Absolutely!

Part of this pride is akin to pride of ownership. Some of the nation's best fighting forces are at Fort Bragg and Pope Air Force Base. Well-known and honored units, such as the Army's only airborne corps, the XVIII Airborne Corps, are headquartered at Fort Bragg. The 82D Airborne Division, perhaps the largest parachute force in the world, also calls Fort Bragg home. In fact, Fort Bragg is known as "Home of the Airborne," although it's Pope Air Force Base that puts the "air" in that "airborne." In 1992, Pope became home to the 23D Wing (The Flying Tigers) of the Air Force's Air Combat Command. Composed of units flying the F-16 Fighting Falcon, the A/OA-10 Thunderbolt II close air support aircraft, and the C-130E Hercules, this composite wing enhances Pope's ability to provide essential support for Fort Bragg's XVIII Airborne Corps and 82D Airborne Division.

Often seen in nightly television

■ *Pike Field, a large parade grounds on Fort Bragg and the site of the annual 82D Division Review, a colorful military pageant.*

■ *Lt. General Gary Luck, a former commander at Fort Bragg, and then-Governor Jim Martin present a red beret to singer Roberta Flack for entertaining the troops after the Gulf War. On more routine days, soldiers can be seen running in unison on Fort Bragg's Long Street.*

newscasts when international events require the intervention of American troops, the runway at Pope AFB is a busy place when it is being used to launch planeload after planeload of soldiers to far-away hot spots. While the rest of America watches on television, Fayetteville sees the up-close-and-personal consequences of such deployments. To Fayettevillians, those departing soldiers and airmen are also neighbors, customers, friends, fellow church members, volunteer coaches, and Boy Scout troop leaders—people whom Fayettevillians know and care deeply about. Fayetteville supports its troops and airmen, wishes them well in completing their missions quickly and safely, and prays for their safe return home—to Fayetteville.

OPERATION APPRECIATION

The greater Fayetteville community sponsors an annual Operation Appreciation, intended to convey the community's thanks to the military personnel and their families, who contribute so much to making Fayetteville a cosmopolitan, economically strong city. Special events, discounts, and sales are offered to military personnel for the week-long event, which culminates with a huge Fourth of July celebration, a Fort Bragg tradition.

This annual celebration evolved from the Operation Appreciation event organized in 1992 by the Fayetteville Chamber of Commerce to welcome home the troops from the Persian Gulf War. The frightening adversity of that war and the trepidation Fayetteville felt for its soldiers combined with the sustained

economic effects of having a large portion of the community gone for a prolonged period of time. With so many personnel from Fort Bragg and Pope Air Force Base transplanted to the Saudi desert, Fayetteville was simply not itself.

One poignant moment remains in the memories of those who attended the Operation Appreciation celebration party at Fort Bragg's Officers' Club in that summer of 1992. Lt. General Gary Luck, then the commanding general of XVIII Airborne Corps and Fort Bragg, had returned from the war and was in attendance at the festive party. Asked to say a few words, the general, a hard-hewn, no-nonsense kind of man, a veteran of the Vietnam War as well, thanked the Fayetteville community for demonstrating its appreciation so visibly. His voice broke for just a moment as he contrasted this warm welcome home to the reception he and his fellow soldiers had received after coming home from Vietnam. Being appreciated, it seems, is very much appreciated by those who wear the military uniform. (General Luck subsequently added a fourth star to his uniform, relinquished command at Fort Bragg, and became the commander of American troops in South Korea.)

LINKS BETWEEN THE MILITARY AND CIVILIAN COMMUNITIES

The business community in Fayetteville has become more than a grateful cheerleader for Fort Bragg and Pope AFB. The Fayetteville Chamber of Commerce's Military Affairs Council is made up of business professionals who are particularly interested in maintaining an excellent relationship with the military installations. They have begun to focus intently on identifying and eliminat-

ing any impediments encountered by Fort Bragg or Pope AFB in meeting its respective mission.

A special task force of the Military Affairs Council keeps the lines of communication open with the leadership at both Fort Bragg and Pope AFB. Members of the task force have traveled to Washington, D.C., to meet with North Carolina's congressional representatives to make the point that Fayetteville wants to remain a place where Fort Bragg and Pope AFB can carry out their missions effectively.

For Fort Bragg, training soldiers is an essential element of meeting its mission. To conduct training exercises and to simulate battle conditions for the thousands of troops at Fort Bragg requires a great deal of space in which to maneuver. With the sustained growth of Fayetteville and Cumberland County, Fort Bragg is concerned with the problems that encroachment on the post boundaries could mean. Homeowners, of course, would rather not live directly in the flight approach path of noisy aircraft or uncomfortably near artillery ranges. The post is working with local planning experts and elected officials to minimize the problems from the points of view of both Fort Bragg and local residents.

The cooperation that exists among Fort Bragg, Pope Air Force Base, and Fayetteville is a wonderful asset that benefits all three communities. Fayetteville reached a milestone in its history, for example, when, in 1993, it hosted for the first time the annual convention of the North Carolina League of Municipalities. Eager to make a memorable positive impression on the conventioneers, who included elected officials and top-level administrators from cities across the state,

Renee Lane is both an Army wife and a business professional. Employed as marketing services manager for Fayetteville Publishing Co., she is a native of Pittsburgh and has lived in other cities in North Carolina.

"I think Fayetteville has developed into a much more livable city than it was even just a decade ago," says Lane. "I like the cultural diversity, knowing people from countries all over the world. But what is especially good about being in business in Fayetteville is that you can still pick up the phone and talk to just about anybody. Those barriers that exist in

■ *Fayetteville beams with pride at military demonstrations, at which one may see huge artillery pieces being fired or paratroopers in motion. At right, a Green Beret soldier checks the ground air speed to determine if it is safe for paratroopers to jump.*

other cities don't exist here. People are very open in Fayetteville—they'll remember a face, and when you're trying to get something done, you'll get lots of cooperation."

Lane has been an active volunteer on the committee that plans Operation Appreciation, the community's thank you to Fayetteville's military neighbors. She feels Fayetteville is very receptive to people who are affiliated with one of the military communities and who have come here from other places.

"Fayetteville as a place to live has a nice feel to it," Lane says. "It's kind of laid back and offers amenities of a larger city all at the same time. It's a hospitable community."

ALMOST 47,000 MILITARY PERSONNEL ARE ASSIGNED TO FORT BRAGG AND POPE AIR FORCE BASE, AND THE MILITARY PAYROLL IN 1994 WAS WELL OVER $1 BILLION.

Fayetteville appealed to Fort Bragg and Pope Air Force Base for help in demonstrating to the 2,000-plus visitors what the Fayetteville community was all about.

Lt. General Henry H. Shelton, a native of North Carolina, was the XVIII Airborne Corps and Fort Bragg commander at the time. Together, the Army and Air Force staged an exercise that provided the military with valuable training—and provided the visitors from the League of Municipalities with a show its members will never forget.

Watching from bleachers at Fort Bragg's Sicily Drop Zone, the visitors were thrilled by the sight of A-10s and F-16s flying overhead, heavy equipment being parachuted onto the drop zone, and hundreds of soldiers parachuting in and "seizing" the drop zone, as they would in combat. Later, the guests convened in a huge hangar at Pope Air Force Base for a dinner catered by the club system at Fort Bragg. The entire day went perfectly.

Fayetteville's mayor, J. L. Dawkins, was a proud man indeed on that October day. Fayetteville's reputation across the state was enhanced by what those visitors saw. And what they saw was not just the action and excitement of a live military exercise; they also witnessed the cooperation between a civilian community and military neighbors that may be unmatched anywhere else in the United States.

Cooperation, of course, is a two-way street, and Fayetteville tries to accommodate the needs of Fort Bragg and Pope Air Force Base as well. Fayetteville responds instantly and sincerely when a need arises at either post. On March 23, 1994, for example, an F-16 fighter jet clipped a C-130 cargo plane in midair. The C-130 landed safely and the jet's pilots ejected, but the plane crashed into a C-141 on the ground. The resulting fireball swept over a group of soldiers on the ground, killing 23 and injuring more than 100. It is at times like these that Fayettevillians mourn along with their military neighbors. Prayer services, help for the families, and public declarations of support and sympathy from the citizens of Fayetteville were immediate and heartfelt.

Lt. General Shelton, the commander of the XVIII Airborne Corps and Fort Bragg as this book is being written, is a past commander of the 82D Airborne Division. During Operation Uphold Democracy in Haiti, General Shelton served as commander of the Joint Task Force.

General Shelton and his wife, Carolyn, live on Fort Bragg in quarters designated for the commanding general. They are highly visible, however, in the Fayetteville community.

Their youngest son attends a Fayetteville high school, as do the other high school-age students who live on Fort Bragg and Pope Air Force Base.

"The military and civilian communities of Fort Bragg and Fayetteville enjoy a very positive, supportive, and mutually beneficial relationship," General Shelton says. "I'm confident our respect for and appreciation of each other will continue to grow in the years to come."

The commanders of Fort Bragg and Pope Air Force Base are often in attendance at social gatherings of the Military Affairs Council. In fact, a huge hangar at Pope has been the setting for some of the most memorable parties Fayetteville has ever seen. One such party had a "Memphis Belle" theme and featured the actual Memphis Belle aircraft displayed in the hangar, appropriately spotlighted as the festivities swirled about it. Whether it's at work or at play, the military communities and Fayetteville are in it together.

One of the more extraordinary events on Fayetteville's calendar is the day-long Pope Air Force Base Open House, which attracts as many as 250,000 visitors to the base to see up close the aircraft, aerial displays, and Fort Bragg's military equipment static displays and to talk to the people who devote their lives to defending our country's national interests.

For some years, the open house was held in conjunction with the Dogwood Festival. The high winds that sometimes occur in April forced cancellation of some of the displays, however, so in the future the open house is expected to take place in October. Whenever it happens, it will certainly continue to be a stellar attraction and undoubtedly

one that will continue to bring more visitors to town than any other one-day event.

A BRIGHT FUTURE FOR FORT BRAGG AND POPE AFB

At a time when the U.S. Army is downsizing, Fort Bragg's future appears to be remarkably stable. Based on the November 1994 Army Stationing and Installation Plan, Fort Bragg's military strength is projected to be 45,459 in 2001, only 357 fewer soldiers than are assigned to the post in mid-1995.

Building activity on the post is one indication that Fort Bragg plans to be functioning well into the next century. The 319-bed Womack Army Medical Center is under construction, at a projected total cost of a quarter billion dollars. Other major construction includes a $29 million barracks complex for the 525th Military Intelligence Brigade, an $8 million company operation complex for the 4th Psychological Operations Group, and a $6.3 million expansion and renovation of the Fort Bragg Youth Center.

As the Army downsizes, Fort Bragg, too, has undergone what is being characterized as a "reengineering" of the way the post does business. Fort Bragg launched a pilot program in March 1995, for example, intended to cut through procurement red tape. Certain Army offices and agencies were issued credit cards to make some categories of purchases locally, eliminating the need for warehousing and stockpiling of basic goods.

Fort Bragg and Pope AFB have always been two of Fayetteville's best customers. This new credit card program should be another one of those mutually beneficial links between Fort Bragg and the business

■ *A young boy demonstrates his gunner technique.*

community; it will enable personnel at the installation to get what they need quickly at competitive prices while infusing more federal dollars into the local economy.

LIFE ON POST AND ON BASE

Though Fort Bragg and Pope Air Force Base are essentially part of the greater Fayetteville community, each installation has its own sense of community as well. Both of the installations are much like small cities, with shopping areas, housing areas, schools, recreation centers, clubs, libraries, movie theaters, medical facilities, and many other amenities of which any community would be proud. The population of each installation includes thousands of family members, as well as the soldiers and airmen assigned to duty.

Both Fort Bragg and Pope Air Force Base have housing for officers and enlisted soldiers and their families. Fort Bragg is a much larger installation than Pope AFB. (Fort Bragg occupies about 150,000 acres of land, whereas Pope covers 153 acres, and Fort Bragg's military population, at about 45,000 people, is nine times Pope's military population.) Consequently, the housing on Fort Bragg is somewhat more diverse, ranging from large brick homes in the Old Post district, currently housing higher-ranking officers assigned to the post, to relatively new modern homes on the post's outer perimeter. On-post and on-base housing is limited; most soldiers and airmen with families live in the greater Fayetteville community.

Fort Bragg proudly displays signs proclaiming its status as an Army Community of Excellence, a designation bestowed by the Army to posts that maintain the best quality of life, gauged by several criteria. The designation, which is prized among posts, comes with extra funding so that further improvements in quality-of-life programs can be made.

Some of the structures in the Old Post district of Fort Bragg are being considered for nomination to the National Register of Historic Places. The entire area is beautifully planned and laid out and is the perfect setting for the main post chapel. The setting for many an Army wedding, the chapel was completed in 1934 and is exquisite, and functional, even today.

AIRBORNE AND SPECIAL OPERATIONS MUSEUM

One of the more exciting prospects on Fayetteville's horizon is the creation of the Airborne and Special Operations Museum, which is expected to be completed in June 1998. The museum complex will be at Fort Bragg and is expected to be a tremendous attraction to the area.

Intended to honor the five decades of accomplishment of Airborne and Special Operations units, the museum is being planned by a foundation, whose board is headed by General James J. Lindsay (Ret.), a former XVIII Airborne Corps commander. Local support, both financial and philosophical, has been extraordinary—one more indication that Fayetteville is proud of its relationship with its military neighbors, Fort Bragg and Pope Air Force Base.

■ *A parachute pulls cargo from the back of a C-130 cargo aircraft. The cargo can be as large as armored tanks and other massive military equipment.*

FAYETTEVILLE CHAMBER OF COMMERCE

In any progressive community, there is a catalyst that brings about positive change. It may be a visionary individual, a dynamic and united government body, or a private sector organization.

In Fayetteville, this catalyst is the Chamber of Commerce, the city's premier business organization. The Chamber's primary mission is to improve the profitability of its members. In the decade of the '90s, however, the focus has expanded to include making Fayetteville a better city in which to conduct business. Certainly, the two concepts are not mutually exclusive; what's good for business is good for Fayetteville, and the reverse is true as well.

All of the various initiatives of the Fayetteville Chamber are divided among its four councils—the Small Business Council, very important because the preponderance of Chamber members are businesses with fewer than 10 employees; the Military Affairs Council, essential in a community whose economic vitality is grounded in the military presence; the Community Development Council, the "heart" of the Chamber's influence in the greater community; and the Membership Services Council, which is responsible for developing the membership base and strengthening the value in Chamber membership.

Through these four councils, the Fayetteville Chamber has exerted a positive influence not only on the profitability of its members but on the greater

community as well. This is evident in several recent initiatives:

• The Chamber was instrumental in the formation of an 11-county regional health insurance purchasing alliance that benefits small business owners, making health insurance a viable option for many small businesses and employees who previously had no affordable access to such coverage.

• Early in 1994, Calvin B. Wells, then the chair of the Chamber, and J. L. Dawkins, the mayor of Fayetteville, convened a blue-ribbon panel to consider ways to reduce litter on the community's thoroughfares and keep the community clean. The strategies developed by that group are being used effectively to deal with this community-wide problem. In 1995, Johnny Lee Dawkins III, the current chair of the Chamber and the mayor's son, continued the war on litter.

• The Chamber conducts a Political Training Institute, a series of sessions to acquaint potential candidates and campaign workers with the realities of campaigning and serving in public office. Alumni of the institute have been elected to various offices in three counties in the region.

• The Chamber also offers leadership training through Leadership Fayetteville, a nine-month-long program that acquaints potential business and community leaders with every aspect of Fayetteville and encourages them to become involved in a leadership role.

These are but a few of the ways the Fayetteville Chamber has influenced positive change in the greater community. An effort of the Chamber's Education Committee, the highly effective Partners in Education initiative, is yet another wide-ranging and long-term project. The recently launched Leadership Fayetteville Youth Academy offers up to 32 high school juniors an opportunity to learn about business and various aspects of Fayetteville and to develop leadership skills and techniques.

Also worth noting is the work of the Business for Arts and Culture Committee. Developed to promote a business relationship with agencies and people in the arts, the committee fosters the development of one of Fayetteville's finest assets, its vibrant and diverse arts community,

Finally, the Chamber is enhancing Fayetteville's quality of life by strengthening the ties between the business community and local government. The Chamber has made a concerted effort in the 1990s to advocate the business position with local government agencies, to monitor issues affecting business that are before these bodies, and to report on these issues to the Chamber membership. The Chamber is also establishing statistics on various quality of life factors to indicate where Fayetteville stands among other cities across the state and nation.

The Chamber has promoted the idea that local government and the business community can be partners in effecting positive change. The Chamber was involved in the passage of school construction bonds in the early '90s; it has lobbied effectively for transportation measures that are having a positive effect on business; and it fosters a healthy relationship with all the local governing bodies, bringing them together for an annual State of Our Community gathering that provides the leaders of each governing body and the Chamber chair with an opportunity to inform the Chamber membership of recent accomplishments. Furthermore, the Chamber provides a standing opportunity at its monthly coffee clubs for these governing bodies to report briefly on issues being considered and recent decisions.

In the early 1990s, the leaders of the Fayetteville Chamber of Commerce made a conscious and far-sighted decision to transform the Chamber into a more visible and effective organization. Faced with the retirement of the executive director in 1990, the Chamber formed a search committee to find a leader who could shift the Chamber into high gear. They ultimately persuaded a young and energetic South Carolinian, J. David Jameson, to take the helm. Experienced in Chamber and economic development efforts, Jameson set about redesigning the organization. His efforts, along with those of the Chamber's volunteers and its highly productive staff, have led to the creation of an organization that has

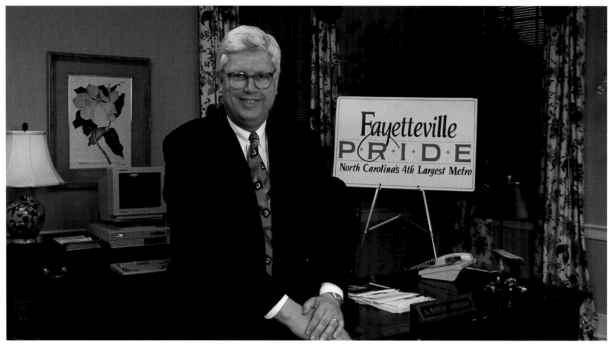

J. David Jamison, president of the Fayetteville Chamber of Commerce

been instrumental in establishing Fayetteville as the state's fourth-largest business market, a city rich with economic opportunity and one its residents—civilian and military alike—are proud to call home.

Recognizing the need to bring the Fayetteville Chamber up to standards that would earn it accreditation from the U.S. Chamber of Commerce, the agency's directors decided to invest in capital improvements that would ultimately benefit the membership. Investment in state-of-the-art office equipment, computers, an improved telephone system, and other business technology was the first step. A period of evaluation followed, in which every aspect and function of the Chamber were assessed by volunteer Chamber members. Strategies to correct deficiencies were devised and action taken. When the Fayetteville Chamber won accreditation from the U.S. Chamber of Commerce in early 1993, the organization was really on its way to being recognized as Fayetteville's premier business organization.

With effective and committed leadership, an active and involved membership that in 1995 is approaching the 1,500 mark, and a highly compe-

tent and productive staff, the Fayetteville Chamber is a model organization. The membership grows annually, a reflection of the value of membership in the organization.

Fayetteville's business leaders are also the Chamber volunteers who chair committees, lead various task forces, and contribute thousands of hours of productive effort to meeting the Chamber's goals and making Fayetteville an ever-better city for business. They are proud to be affiliated with the Chamber. Everyone is happy to participate in success, and success is what the Chamber promises and delivers.

The centennial anniversary of the Fayetteville Chamber is in 1999. By that year, the Chamber hopes to have firmly established Fayetteville as a business and cultural center in North Carolina. No doubt, there will be a year-long celebration in 1999 for the Chamber. Leading the business community of Fayetteville into the next millennium, the Chamber will continue to be a positive force within the greater community, working effectively for an enviable quality of life for all.

FAYETTEVILLE AREA ECONOMIC DEVELOPMENT CORPORATION

The Fayetteville Area Economic Development Corporation (FAEDC) works to ensure Fayetteville's future prosperity. The result of a partnership between the public and private sectors in Fayetteville, FAEDC is charged with pursuing economic growth by attracting new industry and supporting existing industry. Industrial development is a highly competitive process, and FAEDC competes with other cities in North Carolina and throughout the Southeast.

FAEDC has been highly successful in the high-stakes competition for new business and industry. Since 1987, more than 20 companies have worked with FAEDC's professional staff in locating to Fayetteville or expanding pre-existing industrial space in the area.

The annual payroll represented by these new businesses and expansions totals nearly $40 million. This revenue circulates in the community, adding to the economic strength of individual workers and businesses and to the quality of life of all residents.

Informing industrial developers about business and quality of life issues is an important part of FAEDC'S work. Executives ask pointed questions when considering Fayetteville as the destination for their new companies. Questions focus on the composition of Fayetteville's labor pool, transportation routes, wage rates, and amenities as a place to live. How are the schools? What healthcare facilities are available? Are there a range of housing options? Answering these and other questions is just one part of the intricate process of industrial recruitment.

The local government supports FAEDC in its commitment to establish Fayetteville as a competitive player in economic development. The Cumberland County Board of Commissioners unanimously approved an innovative way to solicit new businesses and support existing industry. A special fund has been created from a portion of the increased tax revenue generated by new and expanding industry that can be used to finalize arrangements with industries considering relocating or expanding in Fayetteville. This fund is restricted for use in working with industries that create jobs and increase the amount of money flowing into the community from outside sources.

Left to right: A. N. Prewitt, 1995-96 president; Michael G. Lallier, 1994-95 president; and Danny G. Fore, executive director

THE COOKING CONNECTION

The Cooking Connection is a Fayetteville business that is known, quite literally, for catering to its customers' needs.

Established in 1987 by two enterprising Fayetteville women, Jan Britt and Ann Ashe, the Cooking Connection has become well known throughout the region as a caterer that provides delicious foods for any special event, as well as the accoutrements to serve the food beautifully. The business also can provide, through the hands-on involvement of its owners, the guidance and savoir-faire required to plan an event that will be both elegant and within budget.

Located in Fayetteville's historic Haymount area, the Cooking Connection also offers tasty take-out lunches. Not only are delicious sandwiches available but also soups and absolutely scrumptious desserts. Also available are tasty casseroles that can go directly from the Cooking Connection's freezer to the oven of a busy homemaker who wants to serve a nutritious and delicious hot meal.

On the weekends, the partners in the Cooking Connection are more often involved in catering wedding receptions, including elaborately beautiful but still tasty wedding cakes, or in providing memorable repasts for other social occasions. Reluctant to delegate the work involved in the preparation of their specialties, such as the wedding cakes and other foods for which they have become known, Jan and Ann are quite familiar with very long workdays. Their staff has grown to include seven part-time workers, but both women are involved daily with the business.

Their mutual commitment to hard work and excellence earned Jan and Ann a shared honor: each was named as Outstanding Woman Entrepreneur by Methodist College's Center for Entrepreneurship in 1991. Though both women see their work as an avocation, it is also a business, a responsibility they take seriously. The Cooking Connection is licensed, meets all health department standards, is fully insured, and maintains a membership in Fayetteville's premier business organization, the Fayetteville Chamber of Commerce.

The Cooking Connection is a home-grown entrepreneurial success story for Jan Britt and Ann Ashe—and for Fayetteville, as well.

Ann Ashe (left) and Jan Britt

Quality service is Townsend Real Estate's most important objective. There are larger real estate firms in the Fayetteville area. There are nationally franchised firms. There are firms with construction and development divisions. The Townsend company simply provides thoughtful, committed service to anyone buying or selling property, regardless of size, location, or price range. This satisfies the primary goal set by founder Jimmy Townsend when he opened the company in 1983.

Over the years, Townsend Real Estate has built a highly qualified, responsive roster of sales representatives. The company's ongoing training program keeps agents up to speed on the latest financing trends, changes in the market, and all legal ramifications of real property sales.

From the broker in charge to the receptionist, everyone in the Townsend firm has a working knowledge of every property in the company's inventory. Experienced executives and agent assistants expedite information and transaction processes. Cellular phones, voice mail, call forward, and other up-to-the-minute communication devices—*electronic leashes*—make every agent accessible to clients seven days a week, around the clock.

Townsend Real Estate believes in networking. At the local level, the company and its agents subscribe to market availability listings through the Fayetteville Area Board of REALTORS® and its Multiple Listing Service. On a broader plane, Townsend is the area's only member of the PHH Real Estate Network, a broker-to-broker organization made up of over 54,000 sales associates and 2,100 offices, serving in excess of 500 markets across all of North America.

The prestigious PHH affiliation comes by invitation only. It connects Townsend to PHH Relocation, which handles almost 39,000 relocations annually. This association reinforces Townsend's own Relocation Department, a full-time staff who work with corporate, military, and individual transferees moving to and from the greater Fayetteville area.

Townsend also offers a full-service rental department. An affiliated partnership, Nimocks & Townsend, specializes in commercial real estate sales and management.

As Townsend Real Estate has grown, all departments and affiliates have remained committed to Jimmy Townsend's original goal: first-quality real estate service for the greater Fayetteville area.

© Steven Aldridge

Swayn G. Hamlet & Associates, Inc., is an example of a business that has flourished as a result of Fayetteville's economic development. As a residential and commercial real estate appraisal company, it has been witness to the city's growth since the early 1980s.

It was the recognition of a need for a professional real estate appraisal service in Fayetteville that inspired Swayn G. Hamlet to establish the company. An industrial developer, he realized that Fayetteville was a city with a future when he and his family moved here in 1972. He was certainly right.

Hamlet is appreciative of Fayetteville's excellent economic environment. Having learned the real estate and contracting business firsthand, Hamlet is knowledgeable about both. He is a believer in continuing education, and the list of professional courses he has completed is impressive. Hamlet is certified in North and South Carolina, and his expertise in the finer points of real estate appraisal matters has qualified him as an expert witness in federal court as well as courts in North and South Carolina.

Hamlet points out that the early years of the current decade have been particularly good for real estate and the appraisal business in Fayetteville, and he envisions continued growth in the foreseeable future.

Swayn G. Hamlet & Associates, Inc., is a firm that works hard to maintain the excellent reputation it enjoys throughout the region. Ethical considerations are of the utmost importance to everyone associated with the company, and that commitment, coupled with outstanding professional credentials and experience, have contributed to the company's success.

A generous and committed corporate citizen, Swayn G. Hamlet & Associates is a company that makes time to serve the greater community. Swayn G. Hamlet is a member of the local Chamber of Commerce, has served as president of the Fayetteville Association of Realtors, gave eight years of voluntary service to the Cumberland County Planning Board, and is currently the North Carolina coordinator for the National Association of Realtors, Appraisal Section. It is part of the company's philosophy to be committed to one's family, one's church, and one's greater community.

Swayn G. Hamlet & Associates, Inc., is a business that is happy to be a part of Fayetteville's bright economic future.

Swayn G. Hamlet

CROSS CREEK MALL

f the 16.5 million people who pass through busy Cross Creek Mall annually, many would be astonished to know that as recently as 1973, the site was a bare and empty field. When the mall opened in 1975, with 73 stores, Fayetteville was just beginning to grow into the regional retail magnet that it is today.

Cross Creek has more than 100 stores now—1.1 million square feet of shopping under one roof. And the knowledgeable shoppers who frequent Cross Creek come not only from Fayetteville and surrounding towns but, because of Fayetteville's location on Interstate 95, from out of state as well.

Other retail shopping centers have sprung up around Cross Creek, making the two-square-mile area around the mall the busiest (based on dollars per square foot) retail shopping area in North Carolina. Cross Creek Mall alone generates $200 million annually in sales.

Although the military population provides the mall with a large, relatively affluent, and stable market, the management of Cross Creek takes nothing for granted. Scott Schuler, general manager, says, "We work hard to bring in what our customers want to find." And, in return, Cross Creek enjoys a much higher than national average ratio of sales dollars to square footage.

With a 100 percent occupancy rate, Cross Creek Mall is Fayetteville's prime retail location. Currently "anchored" by four well-known national and regional department stores, Cross Creek is also home to many smaller, nationally known retail chains and specialty shops.

The mall's offerings reflect Fayetteville's youthful population and the preponderance of young families in the area. One often sees young children tossing pennies into the center court fountain, grandparents sharing an ice-cream cone with a grandchild, or young couples window-shopping together.

Besides maintaining an appealing blend of tenants/merchants, the management of Cross Creek values the mall's visual appeal. Periodic interior renovations and refurbishing, as well as landscaping, contribute to its reputation as an exciting and inviting retail center.

Cross Creek Mall has become one of Fayetteville's largest employers. Schuler estimates that as many as 3,000 full- and part-time workers are employed there.

Unlike many malls, Cross Creek tries to accommodate the health-conscious. The mall's doors open at 7 a.m., permitting Fayetteville residents and

visitors to enjoy an early-morning stroll around the mall's internal perimeter before the crowds of shoppers appear on the scene. One such walk is eight-tenths of a mile.

The seasonal displays at Cross Creek Mall are widely known throughout the region and attract many families. An aerial shot of the mall on the day after Thanksgiving invariably reveals completely filled parking lots, while the bustling Christmas shoppers inside fill every wing.

WZFX

For a radio station whose approach to music is characterized as "urban contemporary," WZFX (99.1 "The Fox") is well situated in Fayetteville, North Carolina. With its offices and studios in the heart of the city, WZFX is an uptown success story.

Bursting on the Fayetteville scene in the mid-1980s, WZFX immediately began to capture an increasingly large share of the market. Now consistently at the top of national charts in percentage of market share, WZFX uses its 100,000 watts of power and its state-of-the-art studio technology to reach radio listeners from Raleigh, North Carolina, to Myrtle Beach, South Carolina.

The owner of WZFX is Weil Enterprises of Goldsboro, North Carolina. Weil also is involved in downtown development in Fayetteville, as well as in Raleigh, Goldsboro, and other cities across the state.

Downtown development is part of the company's philosophy. This company believes the heart of any community is its city center. That's why it is here in the heart of Fayetteville.

WZFX employs more than 30 people, including sales consultants, administrative and support staff, and on-air personalities.

Since its beginnings, the station has supported the community through active involvement in events and organizations such as the Fayetteville Dogwood Festival, the Fayetteville Chamber of Commerce, and the Olde Fayetteville Association, to name just a few. Support of Fayetteville State University, the Minority Business Development Center, and the United Negro College Fund has earned WZFX its reputation as a strong ally among members of the minority community. This is important since the minority population comprises as much as 68 percent of he station's listenership.

A blend of the music of such artists as Whitney Houston, Janet Jackson, Anita Baker, and Michael Jackson creates the unique sound that sets WZFX apart from its competitors. In Fayetteville, that sound serves as a rhythmic heartbeat, the very pulse of a city that is on the move.

Bobby Jay, program director

The Radisson Prince Charles Hotel in downtown Fayetteville stands as an imposing testimony to the benefits of renewal and revitalization.

The Prince Charles opened in April 1925. Changing times brought the hotel to what appeared to be an ignominious end a little more than 50 years later, and in 1979 it closed its doors.

Just a decade later, on New Year's Eve 1989, the hotel was enjoying a grand reopening and beginning a renewed reign as Fayetteville's premier downtown hotel. A subsequent affiliation with Radisson linked the hotel with a national reservations system that has contributed to the hotel's consistently high occupancy rate.

By virtue of its architectural distinction and long history, the Radisson Prince Charles is a part of the National Trust for Historic Preservation. Reminiscent of the Mayflower Hotel in Washington, D.C., the handsome hotel is an exquisite example of Adamesque architecture.

The Radisson Prince Charles offers its guests comfort, convenience, and security in beautifully appointed rooms and suites. Amenities include Chloe's, the hotel's restaurant, which is one of the best dining options in Fayetteville, and Babe's, the cozy bar just off the lobby, which is a well-known gathering place. The hotel's eighth-floor ballroom features French doors opening onto the Skyline Terrace. The panorama is of the city Fayetteville is today.

Staying at the Radisson Prince Charles is still an affordable indulgence. Free upgrades to the "Executive" floor are made when

possible, and room rates include a full breakfast in Chloe's and use of the hotel parking lot. Free coffee is served in the lobby each morning, a thoughtful amenity for the traveler eager to get on with the day.

Meeting space and party rooms of various sizes are available, and hotel staff are eager to help plan every aspect of a successful meeting, wedding reception, or party.

FASCO CONSUMER PRODUCTS, INC.

"Our employees are why we are successful." So says Michael T. Fuller, president of Fasco Consumer Products, Inc., and it's evident from the enthusiasm with which he repeats the comment that he really means it.

Fasco has been a part of the Fayetteville manufacturing scene since 1954. Its 260 valued employees make such diverse comfort and convenience products as ceiling fans, central vacuum systems, door chimes, intercoms, electric heaters, range hoods, and ventilators. The commitment to excellence in production methods and customer service is imbued in every employee.

Fasco sells its products to electrical supply and building supply houses, such as Lowe's and Home Depot, and to membership warehouse clubs and building supply chains. Fasco products are everywhere, says Fuller, but rarely do people realize they're buying a Fasco product.

"Because we're not retailers," Fuller says, "we haven't concentrated on building name recognition. You won't see Fasco on your bathroom ventilator, for example—but the odds are that we made it."

Fasco originated in Rochester, New York, in 1911, manufacturing automotive products. In the early 1930s, the company expanded and began making small motors and oscillating fans. Ultimately, three major operating divisions evolved: the Motor Division, the Control Division, and the Consumer Products Division, which became the company that is now in Fayetteville. In 1980, Fasco Industries was purchased by the Hawker Siddeley Group of London, England; in 1991, Hawker Siddeley was bought by BTR Public Limited Company of London, which employs more than 130,000 people in more than 40 countries around the world.

BTR is involved primarily in industrial manufacturing. It directs its capital investment to achieving the best possible design and manufacture of high-performance, cost-effective products.

Fasco Consumer Products, Inc., is pleased to be in Fayetteville, according to Fuller. He cites the abundance of labor and the quality of the people he employs as the reason for his satisfaction.

"They know what the work ethic is," he says.

© Steven Aldridge

"We underwent a restructuring in 1993, and our employees adapted to the changes extremely well,"

Moving away from the standard assembly-line process, Fasco Consumer Products, Inc., has adopted a "just-in-time" philosophy that requires fast responses to customers' orders. Employees are expected to learn more than one function in production, and when they do, their compensation reflects their increased skills. Production is a team effort, which pleases both management and labor. Fasco's customers are even more pleased. They know that the company will respond quickly to fill their orders and that the products they receive will be of excellent quality.

The 1993 restructuring also involved a facelift for the production area of the 340,000-square-foot plant. New lighting, the creation of work stations, and other enhancements made for a more pleasant and more productive work area.

The company's mission statement is prominently displayed in the lobby where visitors are greeted. It reads:

• Fasco will supply quality products to the home comfort and convenience markets while meeting customer needs and earning sound financial returns.
• Fasco will provide a work environment which will attract and retain quality people.
• Fasco will foster profitable long-term partnerships with suppliers and customers.
• Fasco will be a good corporate citizen in our community.

It seems evident that Fasco is fulfilling its mission.

The company is a member of the Fayetteville Chamber of Commerce and an important player in the city's business arena. Fasco Consumer Products, Inc., looks forward to a bright future in Fayetteville, North Carolina.

© Steven Aldridge

The Cumberland County Public Library and Information Center, serving the greater Fayetteville community, is the fourth-largest library system in North Carolina.

With its handsome 80,000-square-foot headquarters library in central Fayetteville, six branch libraries and three more branches expected to be completed by 1999, bookmobile, and law library, the system is and will continue to be highly effective in meeting the informational needs of the community.

Also located at the headquarters library is the North Carolina Foreign Language Center, which has a collec-

diversity of Fayetteville's population, placing the center in Fayetteville was a well-considered decision.

Like all libraries that have evolved from warehouses for books to high-tech resource centers, the Cumberland County Public Library and Information Center is keeping pace with ever-changing information technology. Using a personal computer, one can dial into the library's catalog, check on one's library account, or browse the Internet. A Local Area Network enables library customers at the headquarters library to access extensive reference materials using CD-ROM technology. Coming soon is a Wide Area Network, which will link branches of the library system with these CD-ROM products at the headquarters library.

Whether one is searching for a good read, a past issue of a favorite periodical, a storytelling session for a child, information about community services or literary discussion groups, or simply a quiet, book-filled oasis, the Cumberland County Public Library and Information Center is an excellent place to turn. The staff, in any of the locations, is ready to help you find enlightenment or entertainment or both.

The Strategic Planning Advisory Committee for the library system has developed a five-year plan that articulates the system's mission, goals, and

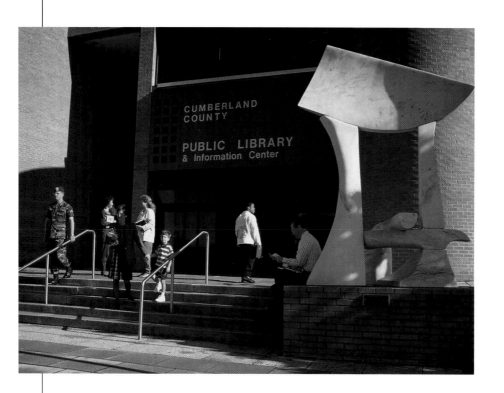

tion of books, videos, audiotapes, and CDs in more than 150 languages. All North Carolina residents may borrow from these offerings. Given the linguistic objectives. The plan will help ensure that Fayetteville's libraries continue to provide excellent service into the twenty-first century.

SMITH BARNEY

mith Barney, founded in 1873, has a local office that has been proudly serving the Fayetteville area since the mid-1950s and is the community's oldest investment brokerage firm. Its mission has never changed, even through several corporate name changes: to provide the best customer service to clients who seek professional guidance in achieving a secure financial future.

Smith Barney's Fayetteville office and its satellite office in Wilmington are overseen by Vice President and Branch Manager Patricia Collie. She points out that Smith Barney enjoys the best of two worlds—the national identity of a long-established and well-known company and the local identity that makes Smith Barney a familiar hometown citizen.

Citizenship is an important concept at Smith Barney.

"We want to be good corporate citizens," Collie says. The local office is staffed with more than 20 financial consultants and support personnel. In combination, these professionals contribute many hours of volunteer time to various community initiatives,

all intended to better the quality of life in Fayetteville. Smith Barney is also recognized as a generous corporate contributor to community fundraising efforts.

The firm recognizes that the presence of Fort Bragg and Pope AFB offers a lot to the economic stability of the entire region. Collie is quick to point out, "We, as a corporate citizen and as individuals, support our troops, embrace their families, and gratefully acknowledge the sacrifices inherent in the life of a soldier." The employees at Smith Barney recognize that the dedication of those troops is unequaled in the world and feel fortunate to have them as friends, neighbors, and clients.

The company prides itself on putting clients' needs "first and foremost," which requires a strong devotion to duty. To help Smith Barney's consultants provide their clients with the best possible service, the company equips its office with state-of-the-art technological tools, including one of the most advanced computer systems in the industry.

During the 1990s, Methodist College became the fastest-growing private college in North Carolina.

In the fall of 1994, Methodist enrolled a record 1,907 students in its day and evening programs, for a gain over the previous year of 206 students. Growing at the rate of 200 students per year, the college is planning several major additions to the campus to accommodate future growth. A capital campaign to raise funds for an addition to the library, a new academic building, and a science annex was launched in 1995.

A 56-student residence hall has just been completed. The Richard L. Player Golf and Tennis Learning Center and an Allied Health Building/Family Medicine Center are now under construction.

Chartered on November 1, 1956, as a senior, coeducational college of liberal arts and sciences, Methodist College was established as a joint venture by the citizens of Fayetteville and Cumberland County and the North Carolina Conference of the United Methodist Church.

In early 1956, a local citizens group—the forerunner of the Methodist College Foundation—offered 577 acres of land, $2 million for initial campus construction, and at least $50,000 in annual sustaining funds. The Methodist Conference accepted the offer, pledging an additional $2 million for campus construction and annual sustaining funds.

The Methodist College Board of Trustees elected Fayetteville attorney Terry Sanford as its first chair. L. Stacy Weaver, superintendent of the Durham City Schools, was elected president in 1957. Construction of the campus began in August 1958. The college opened in September 1960 and graduated its first class in June 1964.

Richard Pearce, a Florida attorney and educator, succeeded L. Stacy Weaver as president in 1973. M. Elton Hendricks, academic dean of Randolph-Macon College, became president in 1983.

With the addition of a physician assistant program in 1996, Methodist will offer bachelor's degrees in 43 fields of study. The curriculum includes the basic liberal arts core, unique concentrations in business (professional golf or tennis management, health care administration, fashion merchandising/retail management), as well as strong programs in English, the sciences, criminal justice, religion, the arts, education, and social work.

M. Elton Hendricks, in his twelfth year as president, has expanded the original vision of "quality education in a Christian atmosphere" by adding new curricula and sports and by seeking national accreditation for new programs.

Methodist College strives to meet the educational needs of both traditional (college-age) and nontraditional (older) students. Eight-week terms of Evening College are offered twice during the fall and spring semesters and once each summer. Generous financial aid packages are available to all full-time students—day or evening. Eighty-three percent of the students attending Methodist College receive financial aid.

The student body is remarkably diverse in age, nationality, and place of residence. Although 41 percent of the students are from Cumberland County, 17 percent are from other North Carolina counties, 38 percent are from other states, and 4 percent are from foreign countries.

© Bill Billings

Methodist College students are a part of a nurturing environment where staff and students experience the joy of learning in a highly personalized, family-type setting. Forty student organizations and 16 intercollegiate sports afford students numerous opportunities to excel outside the classroom and to more fully develop their special talents and leadership skills.

As a member of NCAA Division III, Methodist offers eight intercollegiate sports for men and eight sports for women. Football was added in 1989. The Monarch baseball, golf, and soccer teams are consistently ranked in the top 10 nationally.

Methodist College has a warm and very positive relationship with the greater Fayetteville community, including Fort Bragg. Students and staff are actively involved in civic projects, whether helping with Special Olympics competitions on campus, cutting wood for the needy, collecting clothing or food, or doing guest readings at local elementary schools.

The annual economic impact of the college's 250 employees, $17 million budget, 1,900 students, and 82,000 visitors was approximately $49 million in 1994-95. In 1994, the college made 30 acres of campus land available for construction of the Fayetteville Area Youth Soccer Complex.

Approximately 1,600 of Methodist's 5,800 graduates reside in Cumberland County, where they serve as county commissioners, city councilmen, and leaders in business, educational, civic, and religious organizations.

Reeves Auditorium, an acoustically perfect facility on the Methodist College campus, is at the center of cultural life in the community. It is the venue for performances by the North Carolina Symphony, the Fayetteville Symphony, the Dance Theatre of Fayetteville, and the Cumberland Oratorio Singers, as well as college drama and music groups.

In 1993, the Methodist College Board of Trustees adopted a long-range plan for growth to 2,200 students by the end of the decade. With the completion of new residence halls in 1994 and 1995, Methodist is now able to house 756 students on campus. If growth continues, additional residence halls will be built, increasing the residential capacity to 900 by the year 2000.

The Methodist College family looks to the future with confidence, knowing that "quality education in a Christian atmosphere" will continue to enrich this community and the world beyond.

© Richard Small

North Carolina Communications, Inc., is the largest locally owned communications facility in Fayetteville. The family-owned business has been in existence since 1963, and cumulatively the company's top managers have more than 100 years of experience in the mobile communications field.

North Carolina Communications is a Premier Five Star Dealer for Ericsson GE Mobile Communications, one of the cutting-edge leaders in the mobile communications field. Utilizing the Enhanced Digital Access Communications System (EDACS), the leading trunking system in the world, North Carolina Communications combines the best of radio and cellular communications for the transmission of voice and data. The company prides itself on helping other companies to be competitive in an increasingly challenging business environment.

North Carolina Communications plans to work in conjunction with Ericsson GE and other Special Mobile Radio systems in developing a statewide EDACS. In the future, the company expects to be providing service to increasing numbers of large and small municipalities across the state.

With excellent customer service a company imperative, North Carolina Communications maintains one of the largest inventories of radio parts in North Carolina so as to minimize its customers' downtime. The company also has computerized the repair and maintenance process for individual radio equipment so that a record of every trouble call is maintained. A large test facility, with state-of-the-art electronic equipment, enables North Carolina Communications to maintain any brand of radio equipment to factory specifications.

Guy T. Cayton is the president of North Carolina Communications, Inc., and is ably assisted by his sons, Marty, Tony, and Dean. A deeply held faith in God and a commitment to an uncompromising ethical standard have made the family a strong one. The family name is staked on its commitment to doing business ethically. As Guy Cayton says, "You are dealing with the Caytons when you deal with North Carolina Communications, Inc."

Left to right: Dean, Marty Tony, and Guy T. Cayton

FAYETTEVILLE PUBLISHING COMPANY

The *Fayetteville Observer-Times,* the daily newspaper published by Fayetteville Publishing Company, was founded in 1816, making it North Carolina's oldest continuously published newspaper. As Fayetteville Publishing prepares for the twenty-first century, the company has a long and distinguished history to guide it in serving the citizens of Fayetteville and the 10 surrounding counties.

Owned by the same family since 1923, Fayetteville Publishing is located in a modern, technologically advanced facility on Whitfield Street. There, every day, the *Fayetteville Observer-Times* is written and assembled by a large, well-qualified staff of professional journalists and production specialists. Among the special features the newspaper provides its readers is a full-time Raleigh bureau that covers legislative news from the state's capital, two full pages daily of opinion and editorials, a daily business page, and staff writers who are specialists in health matters and consumer affairs.

Fayetteville Publishing Company contributes a great deal more than a finely written, well-produced daily newspaper. The company is one of the most committed corporate citizens in Fayetteville, quietly nurturing worthwhile initiatives in the community. Among the many charities and community agencies the company supports are an annual Special Olympics fund drive and the Salvation Army's Christmas solicitation on behalf of the community's less fortunate.

Fayetteville Publishing Company has three wholly owned subsidiary divisions that operate out of their downtown Hay Street office. They are the *Carolina Trader,* a weekly classified newspaper; the sales office of the *Paraglide,* the Fort Bragg post weekly newspaper; and the Observer-Times Target Marketing, a division offering direct marketing, printing, and mailing services.

Fayetteville Publishing Company, by providing news and information to the region's citizens, is fulfilling an important role in a democratic society. Anchored in its distinguished history, and equipped to meet the challenges awaiting us all in the future, Fayetteville Publishing will continue to chronicle happenings around an ever-smaller globe, as well as in Fayetteville, North Carolina.

Fayetteville Technical Community College (FTCC) is one of the reasons Fayetteville, North Carolina, is an excellent place to do business.

Now in its fourth decade, FTCC has grown to become a community asset that plays an important role in Fayetteville's economic development. FTCC consistently contributes to the large pool of educated and trained labor in Fayetteville by providing customized training to meet a variety of business and industry needs.

In its effort to support small business in Cumberland County, FTCC recently established the Small Business Center in the Center for Business and Industry. The mission of the Small Business Center is to increase the survivability and profitability of new, small businesses by providing accurate, relevant information and training free of charge.

The Small Business Center offers seminars and workshops designed to address specific topics affecting small businesses. Whatever the needs—a business plan, solutions to employment problems, information on personnel regulations or taxes—the Small Business Center provides accurate, easy-to-grasp material.

© James Carter

The center also provides the services of a business consultant, who is available to personally counsel owners of small businesses. Offering answers and advice, this experienced professional wants to help businesses succeed. The best way to insure this is to provide information, guidance, and encouragement up front.

The center's Resource Center maintains books, videos, and other training material about business. New and aspiring entrepreneurs often come here to learn about specific aspects of operating and owning a business.

In addition to the center's staff of professionals and its materials on the rules and regulations of business, the center offers access to the small business centers of each of the other 57 community colleges across the state via the Internet. This maximizes the business expertise in the community college system, making it available to curious business owners, wherever in the state they may be located.

Another appealing feature that Fayetteville Technical Community College offers to the community is its Decision Support Center, which has proven invaluable to many businesses and agencies. Utilizing TeamFocus software developed by IBM, the center enables businesspeople to conduct electronic meetings. Data indicate that such meetings can reduce the amount of time required to reach a decision by as much as 60 percent.

The Decision Support Center has helped several groups reach important decisions quickly, by enabling the participants to focus on discussing and evaluating issues constructively while removing "personality" factors from the discussion. All TeamFocus sessions provide five major benefits, regardless of diversity in the groups or the variation in objectives:

• *Efficient use of time.* What is more important to a businessperson than time? Everyone at an electronic meeting is able to "talk" at the same time, because their comments are entered electronically on individual screens and displayed on a central monitor.

• *Equal participation.* The timid and the soft-spoken are at no disadvantage here. Everyone has the capability to participate equally.

© James Carter

• *Anonymity.* All participants have the advantage of anonymity. This ensures that the value of an idea is detached from the person who is its proponent, and encourages free-flowing discussion.

• *Ownership.* The collaborative setting imbues all participants, even those whose ideas do not prevail, with a sense of ownership.

• *Permanent record.* There's no chance of faulty memories influencing the action. A printout of the activity of the session is available immediately, so no one needs to be distracted by taking notes.

Fayetteville Technical Community College is also proud to offer access to the information highway. In January 1995, FTCC opened an information highway classroom, funded by a state grant, that links such classrooms across the nation. The classroom is used to receive and transmit class sessions and interactive meetings.

The North Carolina information highway, and FTCC's participation in it, enable the college to provide education to students who would otherwise have to commute great distances. Access to the information highway thus allows the college to further fulfill its mission of providing high-quality educational opportunities to those who need or desire them.

FTCC offers . . .

• More than 60 college-credit programs in areas such as health services, business, technical/vocational studies, and general education.

• Hundreds of adult continuing education classes at convenient locations throughout the community.

• Affordable tuition rates and financial assistance.

CASHWELL APPLIANCE PARTS, INC.

The story of Cashwell Appliance Parts, Inc., is a story of success for Fayetteville and for Jimmy Lee Cashwell, the firm's founder.

Cashwell's experience with a local appliance repair business led to his decision to open the first appliance parts supply outlet in the Fayetteville area. Recognizing the demand for a local distributor of appliance parts, Cashwell founded his business in 1972. Cashwell Appliance Parts, Inc., is now one of the largest appliance parts, distributors in the nation.

Cashwell Appliance Parts, Inc., distributes appliance parts for such well-known and respected manufacturers as Whirlpool, General Electric, Maytag, Frigidaire, Amana, and many more. From the original operation on Fayetteville's Bragg Boulevard, Cashwell Appliance Parts, Inc., has grown to become a company with more than 80 employees in seven locations across North Carolina. Two locations are in Fayetteville: the Distribution Center, located at 3485 Clinton Road, and a branch store at Sycamore Dairy Road. The other locations are in Asheville, Wilmington, Charlotte, Raleigh, and Rocky Mount.

An emphasis on customer service has fueled the company's success. Cashwell's philosophy is simple: Provide the customer with quality parts quickly, and at a fair price. With that approach, it's no wonder the business has flourished.

Another factor in the success of Cashwell is the unique relationship between the owner and the company's employees. Mutual respect and admiration prevail when one talks to an employee or to Cashwell himself. The employees revere Cashwell's caring leadership, while he values their loyalty and dedication to seeing that the business serves its customers well. Some of the employees have been with the company almost since it was founded.

Cashwell Appliance Parts, Inc., is a conscientious corporate citizen

Jimmy Lee Cashwell and the employees of Cashwell Appliance Parts

in Fayetteville, supporting high school job programs and contributing generously to a variety of charitable organizations in the community. The company is a proud member of both the Fayetteville Chamber of Commerce and the Fayetteville Area Economic Development Corporation. Jimmy Lee Cashwell serves on a number of advisory boards, is a past president of the National Appliance Parts Suppliers Association, and is a benefactor of the Boys and Girls Home of Lake Waccamaw. Cashwell is a name in Fayetteville that is held in high regard, personally and professionally.

With the recent acquisition of Hunter Brothers,

Inc., a local company, Cashwell Appliance Parts, Inc., stands poised to expand its services to the Fayetteville community. In addition to a full inventory of appliance parts, Cashwell's will carry flags for public offices and buildings, clocks for schools and other institutions, as well as a complete line of Fasco consumer products, manufactured in Fayetteville.

Cashwell is proud to promote all that is good about Fayetteville. As the city becomes increasingly more prosperous, so will its businesses. This means a better quality of life for all in Fayetteville, a City of Cultures with a Southern Accent.

When patients are treated at Cape Fear Valley Medical Center, they are treated as family. Making a positive difference in the lives of those the center serves has been the goal of Cape Fear Valley since 1956, the year the medical center opened.

With its four stories and 200 beds, Cape Fear Valley Hospital stood tall in 1956 against the expanse of flat fields that surrounded it. Since then, Cape Fear Valley's leaders have continued to build on the vision of the hospital founders, making today's 678-bed medical facility the leading medical provider in a six-county region of Southeastern North Carolina.

As a result of Cape Fear Valley's experience and growth, it is able to offer its patients the best of two worlds: technological advances usually found only in larger cities and the personal touch of a community hospital. Cape Fear Valley provides a variety of specialized medical services, including cancer treatment, heart surgery, neonatal intensive care, pediatric care, nephrology, psychiatric services, and rehabilitation services.

Since 1992, the medical center has provided open heart surgery. Offered in affiliation with Duke University Medical Center, this service is available conveniently close to home for Fayetteville patients

and their families. Cape Fear Valley's Heart Center also provides balloon angioplasty and cardiac catheterization, as well as the comprehensive Healthy Hearts Cardiac Rehabilitation Program. Pulmonary rehabilitation services are available through the Breath of Life Program.

Women's services are another area of expertise at Cape Fear Valley. More than 4,000 babies are delivered each year at the Family Birth Center, making it one of the busiest maternity centers in the state. The 15 new Labor, Delivery, and Recovery suites provide spacious homelike accommodations for expectant mothers. After delivery, both mother and child receive care from a nurse who has been designated as their nurse throughout their stay.

The 21-bed neonatal intensive care unit, the only facility of its kind in the region, offers the highest level of such care. A 23-bed intermediate care nursery and a 60-bed newborn nursery are also available.

Cape Fear Valley is unique in that it provides the community's only civilian pediatric unit. Each private room contains foldout Murphy beds that allow parents to stay comfortably overnight with their children.

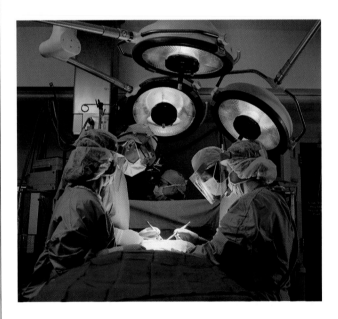

To help alleviate the community's shortage of physicians and to bring medical care to underserved areas of the county, Cape Fear Valley has two pediatric doctors' offices. Physicians care for children at Melrose Pediatric Care and Valley Pediatric Care, both conveniently near the medical center. For the entire family's medical needs, North Ramsey Family Care and Cedar Creek Family Care are available. In addition, Spring Lake Medical Care specializes in internal medicine to meet growing healthcare needs of the county.

Cape Fear Valley has a variety of treatment centers. The comprehensive Cancer Center provides radiation treatment as well as chemotherapy services. Cape Fear Valley also has a magnetic resonance imaging unit with advanced diagnostic capabilities.

Rehabilitation services are provided at Southeastern Regional Rehabilitation Center, a 78-bed facility. This comprehensive, regional center provides treatment for adult and pediatric inpatients and outpatients with strokes, brain injuries, spinal cord injuries, orthopedic injuries, and neurological diseases. An 18-bed brain injury unit as well as a therapeutic gymnasium and pool have recently been added.

Cape Fear Valley offers a full range of psychiatric services at Cumberland Hospital, a 175-bed facility that provides services for ages four through adult. More than 30 specialists provide outpatient treatment at The Behavioral Medicine Center in nearby Bordeaux Professional Center.

Another growing division of Cape Fear Valley is its Emergency Medical Services. With more than 65,000 patient visits annually, Cape Fear Valley's emergency department is one of the busiest in the state. Cape Fear Valley also owns and operates both the Ambulance Service and Rescue Squad, providing doorstep-to-doorstep emergency services. LifeLink enables the medical center to provide a mobile intensive care unit that can transport two critically ill adults, infants, or children.

Other programs and services at Cape Fear Valley include a nephrology unit for inpatient treatment of kidney disease, home health and hospice, pain

management services, occupational health services, and a sleep disorders center. The Patient Services Tower offers three 10-bed intensive care units, one for medical patients, one for surgical patients, and one for heart patients.

All these services are designed to meet the growing medical needs of the Fayetteville community. A public, not-for-profit medical center, Cape Fear Valley ultimately belongs to the tax-paying citizens who live in Cumberland County.

Cape Fear Valley cares about the quality of life in the community. Its staff is dedicated to providing health-care services that the people in the region deserve.

Cape Fear Valley is known throughout the state as the seventh largest hospital in North Carolina, but to the thousands of people in the Cape Fear Region, the medical center is family.

CONSUMERS TITLE COMPANY INC.

Everything about the offices of Consumers Title Company, Inc., bespeaks a cool efficiency. From the tasteful tones of the decor to the motivational posters on the wall, Consumers Title is a company whose focus is its customers. As one of the posters points out, "If we don't take care of the customer, someone else will."

Consumers Title Company is the local agency for Chicago Title, the largest title insurance company in the world, and Consumers Title Company, established in 1985, is the only locally owned and operated title insurance agency in Fayetteville. Linda Lee Allan, president, is proud of that designation, but she is prouder yet of her clients' satisfaction with her company.

And who are those clients? For the most part, they are local attorneys representing buyers and sellers of real estate. The insurance sold by Consumers Title Company protects the lender on any given property, as well as the owner of the property. The company's service is extended on behalf of both residential and commercial transactions.

Consumers Title Company's commitment to client satisfaction manifests itself in a fast turn-around time for paperwork, an attention to detail, a "can-do" attitude that pervades the entire staff—and in Linda Allan's home-baked "thank-you's," which she occasionally sends to her very best customers. She unabashedly admits that her chocolate peanut clusters have endeared Consumers Title Company to the staff of more than one real estate attorney in town!

Allan is generous in praising her staff for the smooth functioning of the business. Aware of the value of being a good corporate citizen, she is often away from the office, serving on several important boards and committees in the community.

"More businesses should realize that contributing to the community also contributes to their own bottom line," Allan says. "A strong, healthy community provides the basis for a strong and healthy business. It's a formula that I know works."

INACOMP COMPUTER CENTER

"We are committed to ensuring the success of our customers," says Johnny Lee Dawkins III, the president of Inacomp Computer Center. "That will ensure our continued success."

That degree of commitment to meeting the customer's needs has built Inacomp into a successful regional business since its inception in 1985. A second location in Myrtle Beach carries Dawkins's philosophy into neighboring South Carolina.

A center for regional businesses in need of computer hardware, software, and networking capability, Inacomp prides itself on the quality of the goods and services it delivers. Novell networking installation and support, Synchronics Point-of-Sale software, and Real World Accounting software are among the brand names Inacomp features. On-site training is also offered for customers who need help in maximizing the benefits of their investment in computer equipment.

Inacomp is a family business, in the best sense of the phrase. Inacomp's major stockholder is Donna Dawkins, the wife of the company president, who also serves as secretary/treasurer of the corporation. (She is also vital in the training aspects of the business.) In addition, Johnny's sister, Dawn Caison, and father-in-law, Richard Palmer, contribute to the successful day-to-day functioning of the company. Even Dawkins's father, J. L. Dawkins, Jr., who has

served several terms as Fayetteville's mayor, is happy to help out occasionally in an advisory capacity.

Johnny Lee Dawkins is keenly aware, perhaps because of his father's example, of the value of public service in building a healthy economic environment in which businesses can grow and prosper. Dawkins served as chair of the Fayetteville Chamber of Commerce in 1995, a commitment deriving from his desire to ensure economic opportunity for others.

Inacomp is located at 2411 Robeson Street, in a building designed by Johnny and owned by him and

his dad. Now employing more than 20 people in Fayetteville and Myrtle Beach, the company is a shining example of how hard work, vision, and commitment can make a dream a reality in Fayetteville, North Carolina.

THE PUBLIC WORKS COMMISSION

When the Public Works Commission (PWC) of Fayetteville was established in 1905, it was responsible for operating the city market stalls and testing weights and measures, as well as providing utility services. Imagine how the Fayetteville community has changed over the years, and it's easy to see why PWC has had to expand its services to keep pace with the growth and prosperity of the Fayetteville area.

PWC has undertaken innovative projects to ensure the most efficient, cost-effective, and environmentally sound utility services for its customers. The water, electricity, and wastewater treatment (sewer) services provided by PWC contribute to the high quality of life enjoyed by local residents. And the availability of these services at very competitive rates helps attract new business to the area. With more than 575 employees and an annual budget of more than $160 million, PWC also makes a significant contribution to the community.

ELECTRICITY

PWC is the only municipal utility in North Carolina to operate its own power plant. The Butler-Warner generation plant keeps customers' rates competitive by providing power during peak consumption hours when purchasing electricity from outside sources is more expensive. With eight gas turbines and one steam turbine, Butler-Warner has a total generating capacity of 285 MW. Called a must-see operation by the American Public Power Association, this PWC facility was one of the first plants ever to be successfully converted for "combined cycle" operation, which means additional power is generated by steam recovered from the turbines' exhaust gas used to run a generator.

Butler-Warner also houses the world's largest thermal energy storage project. This innovative system has attracted worldwide attention because it can cost-effectively increase the plant's capacity by 30 percent in the summer months, when the demand for electricity is greatest.

For nonpeak consumption, PWC purchases power from outside sources at competitive rates. This power is transmitted, through a system that includes 32 substations and more than 2,000 miles of power lines, to 65,000 customers.

WATER

Residents also enjoy a clean, plentiful supply of drinking water, thanks to PWC's water treatment plants. Water from the Cape Fear River undergoes treatment and filtration at the Hoffer water treatment plant before it is distributed. To meet the needs of a growing community, this plant is designed to be easily expanded from its present capacity of 32 million gallons a day (MGD) to 100 MGD. Water from Glenville Lake undergoes the same advanced treatment process at the Glenville Lake water treatment plant. Every year, PWC's two water treatment facilities supply more than eight billion gallons of clean water, through 800 miles of water mains, to 51,000 customers.

PWC's Butler-Warner Generation Plant

WATER TREATMENT

At PWC's Cross Creek and Rockfish Creek wastewater reclamation facilities, wastewater from the community undergoes a series of mechanical and biological processes that remove more than 95 percent of all pollutants. In fact, PWC is the only utility that puts water back into the Cape Fear River cleaner than when it was removed! With a peak capacity of 34 MGD, PWC's wastewater treatment system serves more than 39,000 customers connected to almost 700 miles of sanitary sewer mains.

Biosolids removed during the wastewater treatment process are recycled as fertilizers and soil conditioners. Under a program monitored by state environmental authorities, the biosolids are used on 2,000 acres of Cumberland

PWC's Hoffer Water Treatment Plant

County farmland, including a 700-acre farm owned and operated by PWC.

In all of its activities, PWC demonstrates the utmost concern for the environment and for resource conservation. All five PWC plants meet or exceed the requirements of the Environmental Protection Agency (EPA). Both the Cross Creek and Rockfish Creek wastewater treatment plants have won EPA awards for outstanding operations. The utility is also involved in a program that protects endangered plants and animals. And PWC's consumer information campaigns encourage customers to use water and electricity wisely.

PWC has implemented several programs to support the community. Through SafeWatch, for example, PWC employees use their mobile communications and first aid/CPR training, if appropriate, to help out in emergency situations. Under the Public Watch Cooperative, meter readers and other field service personnel routinely check in on elderly and handicapped customers to see if they need assistance.

Whether it's providing efficient, cost-effective utility services or serving the community, the Public Works Commission plays an important role in making Fayetteville a great place to live and work.

PWC's Cross Creek Water Reclamation Facility

FAYETTEVILLE VETERANS AFFAIRS MEDICAL CENTER

he Veterans Affairs Medical Center in Fayetteville is a beautiful doric structure located on one of the city's busiest thoroughfares. Perhaps what is most memorable about a visit to the site, however, is the meaning of the words inscribed on the sign at the entrance: "The price of freedom is evident here."

Since 1940, the Veterans Affairs Medical Center has been meeting the health-care needs of veterans from across the region. The entire staff, including a dedicated corps of volunteers, are committed to providing the best possible care for the patients.

The original hospital building was designed to incorporate elements of the surrounding community. The building's cupola is formed by a replica of the historic Market House, a Fayetteville landmark. Today, the medical center includes 16 buildings on 47 wooded and attractively landscaped acres.

The VA Medical Center serves a population of more than 160,000 veterans residing in a 21-county region of southeastern North Carolina and a three-county segment of South Carolina. Both inpatient and outpatient services are provided for general medical,

surgical, psychiatric, substance abuse, and hospice care. Other specialties include speech pathology, audiology, rehabilitative medicine, hemodialysis, the fitting of prosthetics, and nuclear medicine. A 10-bed intensive care unit was opened in 1995 as plans for an expanded ambulatory care area move forward. All patient wards have been recently renovated to provide enhanced inpatient services and computer support.

As the complex field of health-care delivery has evolved, so has the Fayetteville Veterans Affairs Medical Center. Patients are assigned to health-care delivery teams, which manage the patients' medical needs by providing direct care or referrals to an appropriate subspecialist. To reinforce its local primary care efforts, since 1992, the medical center has used a well-equipped mobile health clinic to serve veterans in the coastal communities of North Carolina.

As the Fayetteville Veterans Affairs Medical Center continues to evolve in accommodating the health-care needs of veterans, we can expect the medical center to play an important role in Fayetteville into the foreseeable future.

"When most people celebrate a birthday, they blow out candles," says Gary Smith, president of Smith Advertising & Associates (SA&A), referring to the agency's twentieth anniversary in 1994. "You might say we lit a lot of fires instead."

With a record $4.4 million in new billings over that 12-month period, SA&A hit a hot streak that is showing no signs of cooling off. Smith likens the agency's recent achievements to a show business axiom: "To become an overnight success, we had to put in 20 long years."

Perseverance, he contends, is one of the reasons SA&A is where it is today. "We have worked hard to build the kind of reputation we now enjoy. People have been hearing about us for quite some time—and they like what they hear."

The word is spreading well beyond city and state boundaries, carrying SA&A into markets throughout the Southeast. "As we have grown, we have expanded our services," says Smith. "As a result, we have become so much more than an ad agency to our clients." Beyond full-service advertising and marketing, SA&A also offers complete public relations and research departments, which have become so strong that some clients hire the agency solely for the services provided by those departments.

"Without question, our staff is the main reason for the success of Smith Advertising & Associates," continues Smith. "Our department heads have been with the agency for a long time–most 12 to 20 years. They have established a consistent standard of excellence, and we've added a number of bright, talented people who bring fresh perspective to the work."

With a hint of the kind of satisfaction that only triumph can bring, Smith says, "We've come a long way since our rather ominous start in 1974, when our business announcement was placed on the obituary page of the local newspaper."

As busy as the agency is these days, Smith Advertising and Associates is a long way from resting in peace.

Celebrating 20 years of just rewards, the SA&A board of directors, with some of the more than 600 local, regional, and national awards won over the last 20 years. Left to right: Dave Witter, vice president/head of account services; Gary Smith, president; Sonia Hawley, executive vice president/treasurer/controller; Ron Sloan, senior vice president/creative director

MOONLIGHT COMMUNICATIONS

Moonlight Communications is a distinctive video production company with a focus on Fayetteville. A professional partnership between Jan Johnson and Pat Wright, the business hit the ground running in 1993. Since then, it has produced innovative programs for businesses, civic and government organizations, universities, military units, and other clients.

Moonlight Communications is guided by a simple yet powerful vision: to be the company Fayettevillians turn to for creative and effective video productions. Johnson and Wright believe that what sets them apart from similar agencies is that, in addition to their creativity, technological expertise, and marketing skills, they are dedicated to the growth and prosperity of Fayetteville.

Johnson and Wright have promoted Fayetteville's proud heritage, its unique character, its businesses, and its vision for the future. In so doing, Moonlight Communications has established a reputation as an ardent advocate for the city.

Like many focused entrepreneurs, Johnson and Wright are equally involved in every aspect of their business. By combining forces, they more than double the talent and imagination they bring to the creative process. Throughout every phase of production, they both have a single goal in mind—excellence in the products and services they deliver.

Much of Moonlight Communications' success can be attributed to the firm's exceptional service, which is reflected in their clients' satisfaction. Committed to consistently exceeding the customers' expectations, Johnson and Wright believe that going the extra mile for clients is simply a routine part of their daily business.

The video industry is constantly changing, and Moonlight Communications is keeping pace. As a company on the cutting edge, it is poised to be an integral part of Fayetteville's vision for the future.

Johnson and Wright sum up their position this way: "We don't just want to watch Fayetteville's future unfold through a lens. . . . We want to be a part of it!"

In the not-too-distant future, your cable remote unit will enable you to pick a movie from a catalog, play it when you like, pause it, rewind it, or save the rest for later. What's more, you will be able to order pizza with your movie by shopping the "video mall," choose information services for your computer, or even call a friend or member of your family.

The cable wire that today delivers TV programs will tomorrow be the pipe line for the converging media, entertainment, and telecommunications industries. Cablevision of Fayetteville, through its parent company, Time Warner, Inc., is part of that integration. New communications technologies are already being delivered to our schools by cable, along with commercial-free educational programming for teachers and students. The Cable in the Classroom initiative delivers over 500 hours of educational programming each month to every school in Cumberland County, complemented by a free on-line computer service that provides lesson plans and critical viewing tips.

There are many businesses that would like to bring you these new services. But cable is the only high-capacity infrastructure that is available to over 95 percent of the nation's homes. Cable can carry up to 900 times as much information as your telephone wires do and can deliver virtually every sort of advanced communication service imaginable.

Cablevision is preparing for this new era in telecommunications by renewing its commitment to excellence in customer service, to community involvement, and to the latest technology. The office staff received a half-million calls last year and answered over 90 percent in 30 seconds or less. The swift response time to service calls is aided by an ongoing maintenance program and is backed by an on-time guarantee. Over 80,000 customers enjoy up to 43 channels, including four premium services and two pay-per-view channels, plus Music Choice, a 30-channel digital audio service.

Cablevision is making a serious commitment to invest back into the local communities that have contributed to its growth. The Time Warner Volunteer Fund enables employees to obtain funds

for organizations for which they volunteer. Nonprofit groups in our area have received over $32,000 in this manner since 1990. The value of Cablevision's commitment to various educational partnerships exceeds $100,000 annually.

Cablevision of Fayetteville is committed not only to its customers but to the community in general. "We've been serving Fayetteville since 1964," says Alan Spencer, the general manager, "and as we build on our excellent customer service, we'll continue to build on the loyalty and confidence of our customers in us."

At Cablevision of Fayetteville, the future is now!

Campbell University is an outstanding institution of higher education located in Buies Creek, a small residential area halfway between Raleigh and Fayetteville. Proud of its recent designation as North Carolina's safest college campus, Campbell enjoys its serene setting as well as its proximity to Raleigh and Fayetteville and Interstate Highways 95 and 40.

A liberal arts university affiliated with the Baptist State Convention of North Carolina, Campbell has a long and proud history. Founded in 1887, it has grown to become the second-largest private university in the state.

The university offers 50 major areas of study in five undergraduate degree programs, as well as professional and graduate programs in law, pharmacy, education, and business. The School of Law has consistently been among the top schools in the state in bar passage rate. Its graduates had an unprecedented 100 percent pass rate on the 1994 bar exam. The School of Law is also noted for the fact that the movie *A Few Good Men*, starring Tom Cruise as a naval officer, was based on the trial experience of a Campbell Law School graduate.

School of Pharmacy graduates also lead the nation in pass rates on state and national pharmacy board exams. In response to a training and manpower need in the pharmaceutical industry, Campbell has recently instituted an academic program leading to the B.S. degree in pharmaceutical science.

Campbell offers a major in international business, as well as the opportunity to earn both B.B.A. and M.B.A. degrees in just five years. The only university in the nation to offer an undergraduate trust program, Campbell hosts bank and trust officers from the East Coast for the Southeastern Trust School.

Campbell is proud of its award-winning ROTC program, as well as the extension services it provides at Fort Bragg, Pope Air Force Base, Seymour Johnson Air Force Base, and the Marine base at Camp Lejeune. Campbell also has a satellite program that offers B.S. degrees to more than 1,200 students in Kuala Lumpur, Malaysia.

The significant achievements of Campbell graduates can be attributed in part to the fact that more than 80 percent of the faculty of the university hold earned doctorates in their fields, and all classes are taught by the faculty rather than by graduate assistants. Overall enrollment is more than 6,500 students, but the ratio of 1 faculty member for every 18 students is optimum, providing opportunities for the faculty to get to know their students.

Campbell's student body is diverse and active. Students come from each of the 50 states and more than 40 nations. Many of the students receive financial assistance in the form of merit and need-based scholarships.

USA Today has cited Campbell University as one of the top schools in the nation in degree completion among student athletes. A member of the NCAA Division I in men's and women's athletics, the school recently joined the Trans America Athletic Conference.

The university offers a Golf Management Program, culminating in a bachelor of business administration degree. Students need not venture far afield to keep up with their studies. The university's Keith Hills Golf Course is one of the state's top 10 courses and serves as a training resource for the university; avid golfers from all over the region travel to Campbell to avail themselves of the course's lush greens.

Campbell University has earned many accolades over the years. One of the more recent is a tribute from the Newcomen Society of the United States, an educational foundation chartered under the Charitable Law of the State of Maine for the study and recognition of achievement in American business. In 1993, the Newcomen Society honored Campbell, along with Princeton University and the University of Notre Dame, for their contributions to the free enterprise system.

Campbell is an important influence in the Fayetteville area, as well as in the region and the state of North Carolina and will continue to be so as the university continues its commitment to providing an excellent education.

Fort Bragg's Womack Army Medical Center is where the military and medicine meet.

Womack is at the forefront of military medicine delivered with a customer-service focus and is an innovator in providing primary health care to more than 163,000 military-related beneficiaries in the surrounding 40-mile area.

With one eye on world situations, Womack staff are always ready at a moment's notice to provide health care to troops at home or anyplace else in the world.

Womack's staff of close to 2,000—about half military and half civilian—work in close collaboration with local civilian health-care professionals. The three largest health-care areas—primary care, orthopedics, and women's health—reflect the diversity of the patient population, many young families having children and Fort Bragg being home of the Airborne.

Womack is the only Army medical center to be named after an enlisted soldier, Private First Class Bryant Homer Womack, a native of North Carolinia who was killed during the Korean conflict. He was awarded the Medal of Honor for his courageous actions.

Womack Army Medical Center was officially activated as a medical center October 10, 1991. Prior to activation, it was a community hospital that was built in 1958 and had a long, distinguished history. The first medical buildings at Fort Bragg were built in 1918, and medical care has been offered continuously ever since.

To provide continuing quality care in a state-of-the-art facility, Womack began construction on a new $250 million medical center in 1992. The new Womack is scheduled to open in late 1999 on a 163-acre site one-half mile from the current medical center.

The old facility will be put to good use. Plans are being made to use portions of it for medical care and portions to provide for Womack's most important customers—active-duty service members who must be fit to fight and ready to deploy to protect our nation or to provide humanitarian relief to areas stricken by disaster.

The new Womack will be close to one million square feet—twice the size of the current facility, or approximately the size of Cross Creek Mall in Fayetteville.

The new medical center will include a six-story inpatient tower on the east side, a three-story ancillary building in the center of the complex, and a two-story clinical wing on the west side.

Plans call for a 287-bed facility. The medical center will provide continued quality care and access to beneficiaries by enabling more medical and specialized resources to be brought to Fort Bragg. New services will include cardiology, hematology-oncology, plastic surgery, complicated obstetrics, child and adolescent psychiatry, pulmonology, endocrinology, thoracic surgery, and a level II nursery.

© Sandy Neill

Capt. James Quigley, head nurse, right, goes over scheduling procedures with Sgt. Shane Wagner, Department of Social Work, at Womack Army Medical Center's Male Medicine Ward.

The current Womack Army Medical Center was dedicated in 1958. Once the new $250 million medical center is compleleted in late 1999, this building will be used not only for some medical clinics but also to provide more services to Fort Bragg soldiers.

In addition, Womack's Robinson Health Clinic in the 82nd Airborne Division area opened for the more than 30,000 soldiers and their families in February 1995 to meet their outpatient needs. The $5 million clinic is named after Gen. Roscoe Robinson, Jr., the 82nd's first African-American commander.

Two other clinics are planned that will provide outpatient health care to active-duty Fort Bragg families.

A $12.2 million clinic for the 1st Corps Support Command is scheduled to be built in the COSCOM area east of Bragg Boulevard starting in 1997. And an $11.6 million clinic in the Smoke Bomb Hill area is scheduled to begin construction in 1997 near the main noncommissioned officers' club.

Womack's commitment to Fort Bragg and surrounding counties goes beyond patient care. Womack's staff volunteer to teach health education classes, speak at civilian and civic organizations, and work with HealthCare 1999 (HC 99) task forces.

HC 99's vision is to create a coordinated health-care system in collaboration with regional medical institutions. Womack staff gives back to the community in many ways.

Another well-known program is CHAMPUS, or the Civilian Health and Medical Program for the Uniformed Services. It was formed to help with the medical costs of beneficiaries (not active-duty soldiers, whose health needs take first priority at military treatment facilities) who live outside the military hospital area, cannot get to a military hospital in an emergency, or need treatment that is not available in military hospitals. CHAMPUS counselors are available at the medical center to answer questions.

TRICARE, a Department of Defense-managed health-care program, is scheduled for implementation at Fort Bragg in 1997. It is a wellness-based health-care program with an emphasis on quality and access at a reasonable cost to the community.

The new $250 million Womack Army Medical Center is scheduled to open for patient care in late 1999. Twice the size of the current Womack, the new facility will blend harmoniously with the traditional buildings on Fort Bragg's Main Post. The great size is subdued through the separation of the primary building components, creating a campus-like atmosphere. The Clinic Mall Building of the new Womack (below) incorporates the latest concepts in ambulatory facility design.

As medicine moves from a sickness-based model to a wellness-based one, military medicine remains in the forefront of technology.

Womack is home to the Army's largest family practice residency program and, on average, graduates 10 residents per year. As the nation moves more toward primary care providers, Womack is providing the training that is needed.

In addition, Womack has many memoranda of affiliation. In any given month, more than 300 students, residents, and interns from prestigious medical institutions such as Duke University Medical Center and Walter Reed Army Medical Center are training with Womack staff.

A mental health contract was awarded in April 1995 for the Fort Bragg catchment area, which will enhance mental health care for all eligible CHAMPUS beneficiaries. FHC Options of Virginia was awarded the more than $63.7 million five-year contract.

The mental health contract includes care for CHAMPUS-eligible adults and patient cost-sharing requirements. The contractor will also provide a local resource center for clients.

The mental health contract is one more way Womack Army Medical Center will continue its commitment and tradition of health-care excellence into the twenty-first century.

Womack Army Medical Center is dedicated to providing the finest health care possible to the most highly trained and motivated service members in the world.

TRICARE is a new triple option program that offers CHAMPUS-eligible beneficiaries more choice in their health care. TRICARE Standard is the same as CHAMPUS, TRICARE Extra lowers the cost when patients receive civilian care from a Preferred Provider Network, and TRICARE Prime—the only option requiring enrollment—is the health maintenance option.

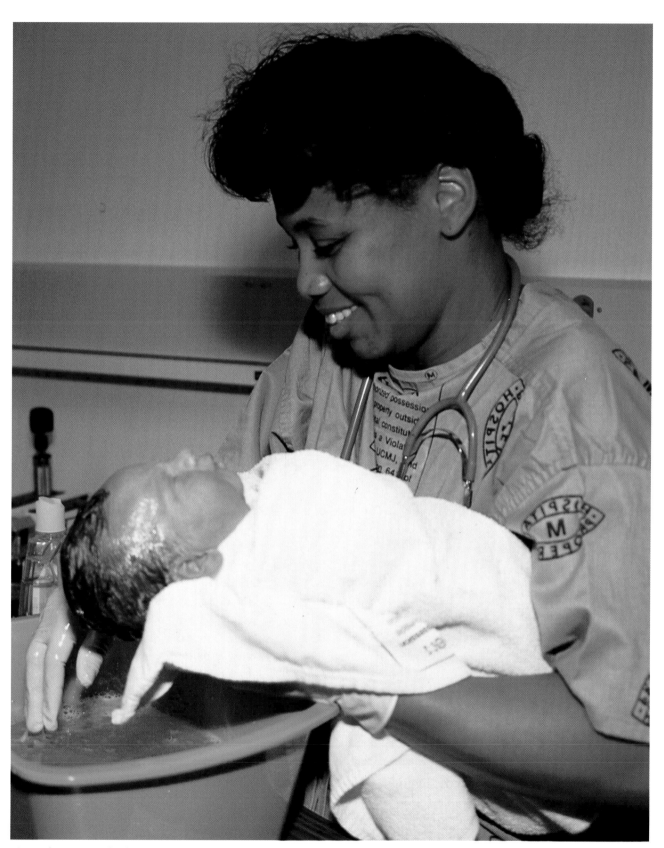

Capt. Gloria Murray, head nurse, gives little Eric Fleek, only 30 minutes old, his first bath at Womack Army Medical Center's Newborn Nursery.

NORTH CAROLINA NATURAL GAS CORPORATION

North Carolina Natural Gas (NCNG) proudly serves natural gas to over 135,000 customers in south-central and eastern North Carolina, including almost 30,000 homes in Fayetteville and Cumberland County. Many of the best homes in Fayetteville have the natural gas advantage for comfort, convenience, and low operating costs.

NCNG also makes natural gas available to more than 65 other towns and communities through 21 customer service offices with a staff of 530 dedicated employees. The company is the largest publicly held corporation with headquarters in Fayetteville, and its stock is traded on the New York Stock Exchange.

In addition to the homes and apartments that are served with natural gas, many commercial and industrial facilities in the Fayetteville area benefit from using economical, clean-burning natural gas.

Kelly-Springfield, whose Fayetteville tire-manufacturing plant is the world's largest, depends on natural gas for most of its process heating needs. In addition, Fort Bragg uses natural gas extensively in its facilities and operations.

In 1994, NCNG's annual sales and transportation volumes totaled 47 million dekatherms. That volume, approximately 70 percent of which was delivered to industrial plants, is enough natural gas to meet the needs of 600,000 homes.

NCNG was founded in 1955 to deliver natural gas to industrial plants, to the four municipal gas systems owned by the cities of Greenville, Monroe, Rocky Mount, and Wilson, and to Tidewater Gas Company, which was subsequently merged into NCNG. The company has built transmission pipe lines and connected distribution systems from Albemarle to Wilmington, northeast from Pembroke through Fayetteville, Goldsboro, Rocky Mount, and other towns, and to the North Carolina-Virginia border near Roanoke Rapids.

The construction of NCNG's original 650-mile pipe line during 1958–59 helped make eastern North Carolina an attractive location for new industry. Today, NCNG's high-pressure transmission pipe line has grown to nearly 1,000 miles with over 2,500 miles of distribution mains.

The company formed its first subsidiary, NCNG Exploration Corporation, in the 1970s to augment its gas supplies with new gas from drilling projects. A second subsidiary, Cape Fear Energy Corporation, was formed in 1980 to invest in additional exploration and drilling programs. Recently, Cape Fear Energy, a natural gas marketing company, has been formed to service large-volume industrial customers that wish to purchase gas directly at the wellhead. After the gas is delivered to North Carolina by an

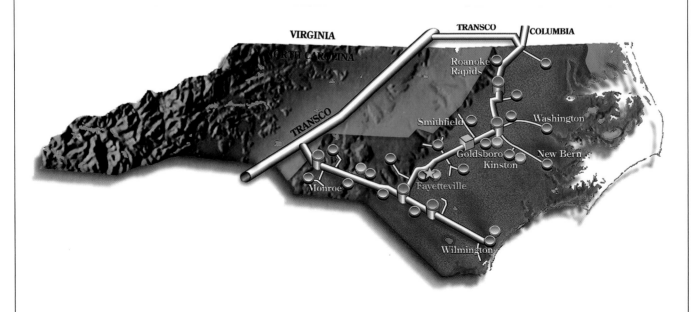

interstate pipe line, NCNG transports the gas to the customers.

The ever-increasing demand for natural gas over the years has required NCNG to increase its gas supply contracts several times. Natural gas is delivered to NCNG by two interstate pipe line companies, Transcontinental Gas Pipe Line Corporation and Columbia Gas Transmission Corporation. Transco delivers natural gas to NCNG at points near Davidson and Pleasant Hill, while Columbia has a single delivery point at Pleasant Hill. Five compressor stations move gas through the pipe line system and are operated as needed to increase the company's delivery capacity, especially during peak operating periods on cold winter days.

In October 1984, the company began its largest undertaking since the initial pipe line was completed: the construction of a billion-cubic-feet liquefied natural gas (LNG) storage facility near the center of its pipe line system. The LNG plant, completed in the summer of 1986 at a cost in excess of $20 million, has the capacity to meet increased customer requirements during the coldest winter periods. Natural gas in the liquefied state uses only 1/600th of the space required when it is in a vapor state in the pipe line. Modifications are currently under way to double the delivery capacity of the LNG plant from its original design.

For Fayetteville area homeowners and businesses that are not located on a natural gas main but that want the advantages of a clean-burning competitive fuel, NCNG's Propane Division has a

© Cramer Gallimore

full-service operation. Over 8,000 customers currently use propane for space heating and other energy needs.

NCNG's employees have enjoyed serving the energy needs of consumers in the Fayetteville area for over 35 years. They look forward to participating in the continued growth of the community in the years ahead.

Cape Fear Supply/Comtech, Inc., is an independent, family-owned business in Fayetteville that offers top-quality lumber, building materials, and design services to professional builders and contractors as well as to the do-it-yourselfer and home remodeler.

The firm has clearly made tangible contributions to Fayetteville's growth and development; in the 70 years the company has been in existence, it has literally helped build the community as well as a successful business.

Although located under one corporate "roof," the business occupies a sprawling 15-acre site, encompassing several facilities. It consists of an engineered truss manufacturing facility; a door, window, and millwork assembly plant; a hardware center; a lumber, plywood, and materials distribution yard; a commercial construction materials division; and a comprehensive kitchen products and design operation, complete with a cabinet and countertop shop. Cape Fear Supply/Comtech is located in Reilly Road Industrial Park, proximate to the area of Fayetteville experiencing the most rapid and extensive growth.

Cape Fear Supply/Comtech attributes its growth and success to its dedicated corps of more than 100 employees. By working hard to improve materials delivery, or using computer technology to expedite and improve services, or thoughtfully educating a customer on new materials and building techniques, the employees of Cape Fear Supply/Comtech provide a level of customer service that sets the company apart from its competitors.

Located adjacent to Fort Bragg's "back door," Cape Fear Supply/Comtech is a staunch supporter of Fayetteville's military community. The company is proud to have provided materials for many of the military's building projects.

Like Fayetteville itself, Cape Fear Supply/Comtech faces a bright and challenging future. As an independent building materials supplier, the company adapts quickly and reacts aggressively to changes in what is sometimes a volatile industry. The company will be a part of the Fayetteville business landscape for some time to come.

BELK

In 1888, 25-year-old William Henry Belk opened a small store in Monroe, North Carolina. Belk's store was a success; in fact, it did so well that three years after opening, Belk persuaded his brother, John, to join him in the business.

Their reputation for honest dealing won many customers and laid the foundation that enabled Belk stores to expand rapidly throughout the Southeast. Loyal employees were offered the chance to establish new stores under the Belk name and their own. The descendants of these early "partners" continue to share an interest in many of the Belk corporations today, which operate 270 Belk and Leggett stores in 14 southeastern states from Delaware south to Florida and west to Texas.

This method of expansion brought John W. Hensdale to Fayetteville in 1926 to establish the Belk-Stevens department store. Three years later, Hensdale became a partner and the store's name was changed to the Belk-Hensdale Company.

Belk-Hensdale prospered and grew, expanding into 13 other North Carolina communities before Hensdale's retirement in 1971.

The Belk Fayetteville Group continues to grow in size and influence, and recently it merged with the Rocky Mount-based Belk group of stores. The Group Office and Service Center, located in Fayetteville, now operates 30 stores in 24 North Carolina communities, including three stores in Fayetteville: at Cross Creek Mall, Tallywood Shopping Center, and Eutaw Village.

Associates of the Belk Fayetteville Group have long been active in the civic affairs of the communities they serve. John W. Hensdale was instrumental in the establishment of Methodist College and provided leadership and financial support to many local causes. More recently, Belk has provided support for such local institutions as the Cape Fear Regional Theater, the Cape Fear Botanical Gardens, the Museum of the Cape Fear, and the Fayetteville Museum of Art.

MID-SOUTH INSURANCE COMPANY

Mid-South Insurance Company, which was founded in Fayetteville, markets, underwrites, and services health, accident, and life insurance policies. The company's executive offices are housed in a handsome three-story home office structure in Fayetteville. Sales offices are maintained in Fayetteville, Greensboro, Charlotte, and Columbia, South Carolina.

Because Mid-South is a home-grown company, founded by Walter B. Clark in 1960, Fayetteville has a proprietary pride in its success. In its 35-year history, the company has grown steadily in assets and influence, and it is one of two Fayetteville-based companies whose stock is traded publicly.

Clark remains actively involved in the company as chairman of the board of directors, chief executive officer, and treasurer. The passage of time has confirmed Clark's instinct that Fayetteville was the right place to establish Mid-South. When the doors of the company opened in May 1960, he was assisted by a secretary. Now, Mid-South employs about 100 people and is further represented by more than 2,000 independent insurance agents in 28 states as well as the District of Columbia and the U.S. Virgin Islands.

In addition to the revenues generated by the underwriting and sale of insurance policies, the company derives income from its investments. Choosing not to invest in real estate or mortgage loans, Mid-South opts for a conservative investment strategy that has served the company's policyholders and shareholders well over the years. By investing primarily in bonds of the U.S. government or agencies of the U.S. government or corporate bonds rated "A" or higher, Mid-South has ensured that its bond holdings are of investment grade quality.

As with any business involved in health care, Mid-South Insurance Company is concerned with cost containment. As health-care costs rise, so must insurance premiums. In response to this challenge, Mid-South has developed Accountable Health Networks, which bring primary-care physicians, specialty physicians, and hospitals into exclusive partnerships with the company, thereby offering significant discounts in exchange for a large volume of patients. The company anticipates that Accountable Health Networks will represent an increasing percentage of group medical premiums and will help ensure the stability of Mid-South's accident and health loss ratio.

Walter B. Clark says that the company's success has been enhanced by the talented, loyal employees who have worked for Mid-South. It has been a particular pleasure, Clark says, to see young people join the company and to observe them develop into top-notch insurance professionals, capable of meeting the challenges that tomorrow will hold for the insurance and health-care industries.

Locally, the company is a member of the Fayetteville Chamber of Commerce and the Fayetteville Area Economic Development Corporation.

The board of directors of Mid-South Insurance Company: (standing left to right) Kenneth W. Cherry; Wilson F. Yarborough, Jr.; Donald G. Walser; Alfred E. Cleveland III; Graham B. Blanton; Edward M. Hicklin; Dan R. Thomason; (seated left to right) Jack R. Lindley; N. Hector McGeachy, Jr.; Walter B. Clark; and Donald W. McCoy. W. A. Bissette was not present.

Walter B. Clark and Graham B. Blanton

Mid-South Insurance Company stock is held to a large extent by its original shareholders, people who purchased stock in 1960 when the company was formed. The stock is now listed on NASDAQ.

Mid-South Insurance Company stands today as evidence that business success can result from the combination of a good idea, the efforts of competent, loyal professionals, and the healthy economic setting of a particular community. Fayetteville is proud of Mid-South Insurance Company and looks forward to its continued success in the twenty-first century.

PI, Inc., D/B/A/ Professional Investigations of Fayetteville

Fayetteville and southeastern North Carolina businesses concerned about loss prevention and the internal integrity of their companies have an ally in Professional Investigations.

Client confidentiality is a top priority of this thoroughly professional organization. The firm, established in 1978, has quietly built a solid reputation for delivering results to its clients in a cost-effective manner. Professional Investigations and its investigators are fully licensed, bonded, and insured.

Professional Investigations uses a full range of the most modern equipment and techniques to conduct comprehensive investigations, undercover operations, and surveillance. The firm also offers loss-prevention surveys to identify and avert potential problems.

By providing its corporate clients with information, documentation, photographs, videotape, physical evidence, and testimony, Professional Investigations enables its clients to make intelligent, fully informed decisions concerning personnel actions and loss prevention.

Among the firm's additional capabilities are developmental, verification, and background investigations; consulting services; evidence collection; and a service that can determine employee honesty, product knowledge, attitude, and adherence to company policy. Unfair business practices, workers' compensation, and insurance fraud investigations are also available. Not wanting to overlook the individual's needs, Professional Investigations offers a full range of personal services as well.

William L. Kiker III, the president of Professional Investigations, holds a B.S. in social science and is close to completing an M.A. in the administration of justice. An experienced college instructor in the criminal justice field, he is court-certified as an expert investigator and photographer and has extensive contacts in the law enforcement and legal communities.

Robert C. Williams, Jr., secretary/treasurer of Professional Investigations, holds a B.A. in history and an M.A. in the administration of justice. He, too, is an experienced college instructor in the criminal justice field. The cumulative experiences of the company's officers endows the firm with more than 75 years of investigative expertise. Add in the experience of its investigative staff and employees, and the total is more than 125 years of experience on which the company can draw.

Professional Investigations is a long-time member of the Fayetteville Chamber of Commerce, the American Society for Industrial Security, International, and many other professional organizations. The company is located in the historic Haymount section of Fayetteville and is proud to be a part of the city's and region's established business community. Professional Investigations looks forward to participating in Fayetteville's bright future.

FIRST UNION NATIONAL BANK

The Fayetteville office of the First Union National Bank of North Carolina is part of the Charlotte-based First Union Corporation. On June 19, 1995, First Union announced a definitive merger agreement with First Fidelity Bancorporation that would create the nation's sixth-largest bank holding company, based on total assets of approximately $124 billion. Pending approval, the groundbreaking merger will create an East Coast banking leader serving 10.5 million customers through 2,000 offices in 13 states, from Florida to Connecticut.

Mary Holmes, city executive for First Union in Fayetteville, says the bank's aim is simple: Provide the *best* financial services to its customers, whether they are large companies, small businesses, or individuals needing a mortgage or checking account. A native of Fayetteville, Holmes says First Union provides Wall Street services with hometown convenience and a personal touch.

First Union is well positioned in Fayetteville with convenient locations and state-of-the-art services. In addition to traditional banking services, First Union is a leader in computer banking services, including "Cyber-Banking." A streamlined organization, First Union has reduced the turnaround time on a commercial loan application to as little as three days.

First Union is supportive of the Fayetteville Chamber of Commerce and the Fayetteville Area Economic Development Corporation and a member of both organizations. First Union's leaders know that a healthy economic base and excellent quality of life are essential to Fayetteville's continued growth and development.

The bank is proud to have played a part in Fayetteville's sustained economic growth and has been a responsible and generous corporate citizen. Focusing on addressing needs in public education, First Union is a Partner in Education with the Cumberland County schools and touches the lives of as many as 6,000 students each year. Sponsoring the Banks in Schools and WhizKidz programs, First Union is committed to providing meaningful learning experiences for Fayetteville's children.

This commitment to education extends to First Union's personnel policy. The bank provides each employee with up to four hours of paid time away from work each month to attend parent/teacher conferences, special programs, or simply to volunteer at a school.

As a strong financial institution and as an influential corporate leader in the community, First Union National Bank is investing in Faytteville's future.

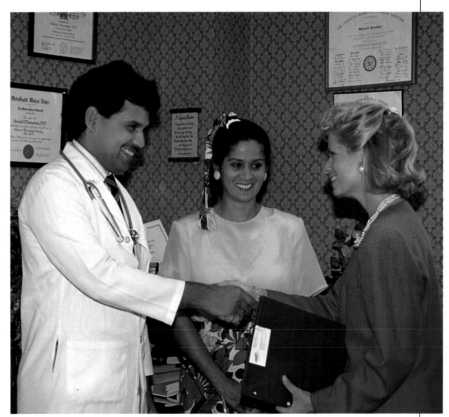

First Union's Kerri Hurley delivers mortgage information to Dr. and Mrs. Shirish Devasthali of the Blood and Cancer Clinic.

Cellular One has been an exciting and innovative presence on the Fayetteville scene since June 1987, when cellular service was first introduced to the city. Since then, Cellular One has kept pace with the rapidly developing technology in the telecommunications industry.

Cellular One transmits voice, data, and even video signals via a nationwide network that links the United States and Canada into one "seamless" system. The company, owned by telecommunications giant GTE, stands ready to accommodate future

munication needs of any business, large or small. At the same time, the company offers a variety of air-time usage plans and equipment that are ideal for the individual consumer who wants cellular service for reasons of security or convenience.

A self-assessment by the company in 1995 stemmed from its commitment to provide "quality" in all aspects of its interactions with its customers. This self-scrutiny, which was based on the Malcolm Baldrige National Quality Award criteria, led to an internal consensus on the definition of quality as it applies to customer service and a recommitment within every department, by every employee, to maintain a standard of excellence that would set the company apart. More than a nebulous concept, quality at Cellular One involves meeting specific standards and maintaining those standards under all circumstances.

Cellular One is among Fayetteville's most involved and generous corporate citizens. Through the Partners in Education program, the company has provided equipment and service gratis to the Cumberland County schools' resource officers, to be used on activity buses and in various administrative capacities. The company annually underwrites a production at the Cape Fear Regional Theater

technological developments that will make it possible for consumers to communicate in ways that were once thought impossible.

Priding itself on being a company that is "easy to do business with," Cellular One caters to the corporate customer. With cost-effective corporate plans designed for as few as five phones or as many as several hundred, Cellular One is able to meet the com-

and has long been a sponsor of the Dogwood Festival. Cellular One is also a sponsor of Operation Appreciation, the Fayetteville community's "thank you" to the military.

As the twenty-first century approaches, with all the exciting new technology that it is certain to bring, Cellular One will continue to be a leader in bringing that technology to Fayetteville.

VILLAGE SURGICAL ASSOCIATES

Village Surgical Associates is composed of six board-certified surgeons, including Fayetteville's only vascular surgeon and surgical intensivists, as well as specialists in general, thoracic, and pediatric surgery. Established in 1979, Village Surgical Associates has evolved into the largest general surgery practice in eastern North Carolina. It is proud to use the latest in surgical techniques and laparoscopic surgery.

The surgeons of Village Surgical Associates are privileged to be able to use the most advanced laparoscopic operating room in the world. Carolina Laparoscopy, a division of Village Surgical Associates, is largely responsible for the design of the operating facility, located at Cape Fear Valley Medical Center. The operating room incorporates the most advanced equipment and design considerations. With one of the nation's largest practices experienced in minimally invasive hernia repairs, Village Surgical Associates is pleased to host visiting physicians who come to Fayetteville to observe the procedure.

The surgeons of Village Surgical Associates perform most of their procedures at Fayetteville Ambulatory Surgery Center, Cape Fear Valley Medical Center, and Highsmith-Rainey Hospital. Minor procedures are performed at Village Surgical's office.

Village Surgical Associates contributes much back to the community that has helped its practice flourish. Involvement in residency teaching programs, the sponsorship of Cape Fear Regional Theater productions, the support of events staged by the Olde Fayetteville Association, and participation as individuals and corporately in many other organizations demonstrate Village Surgical Associates' commitment to the community and to improving the quality of life in Fayetteville.

In an era when everyone is concerned about the escalating costs of health care, Village Surgical Associates is equally concerned about maintaining high medical standards. The practice is committed to providing high-quality, cost-effective surgical alternatives for patients, utilizing the most advanced medical techniques.

Village Surgical Associates will be an important player as Fayetteville progresses in becoming a regional health-care center. With its well-established reputation, the practice undoubtedly will be an integral part of the business and health-care community in Fayetteville well into the twenty-first century.

Not only is the Prudential John Koenig, REALTORS® Fayetteville's largest real estate company, but it also is ranked among the nation's top 250 real estate brokerages.

The history of the company is a Fayetteville success story. John Koenig, a retired Army officer, began a part-time real estate career in 1972. After serving as sales manager in a local real estate company, Koenig bought the company and began its ascent to the national standing it holds today. In 1976, the

John Koenig

company gained the top market position in the Fayetteville area, a distinction that has yet to be relinquished. In 1989, the firm became North Carolina's first Prudential Real Estate affiliate. The company maintains three offices in Fayetteville and one in Jacksonville.

A diversified company, it is building and developing residential neighborhoods throughout the region. The Prudential John Koenig, REALTORS® sign is a familiar one throughout Fayetteville; entire neighborhoods have resulted from the company's efforts to provide high-quality custom-built housing for its clients.

The Prudential John Koenig, REALTORS® embarked in the mid-1990s on a development project in neighboring Harnett County that promises to change the face of the region. Northridge Plantation is a 1,700-acre development that will ultimately include thousands of new homes, as well as the commercial support services required to sustain a residential population of that magnitude.

The company is particularly focused on accommodating the needs of corporate clients. The firm's relocation center works closely with companies that may be transferring employees to or from Fayetteville, as well as with professional associations involved in the recruitment of physicians and other medical professionals into Fayetteville's burgeoning health-care community.

Today, John S. Koenig works along with his father and the many other employees of the company in providing first-class real estate services to the greater Fayetteville area and southeastern North Carolina. The company is looking forward to leading the way for years to come as Fayetteville grows and meets its potential as a high-quality metropolitan community.

AMERICAN UNIFORM SALES, INC.

American Uniform Sales, Inc., was established in Fayetteville in the mid-1970s as a two-person company. Perhaps the most auspicious aspect of the firm's beginnings was its motto: "Quality and Service." In the intervening decades, American Uniform Sales, Inc., has fulfilled that motto, growing and developing to become the supplier of uniforms to such well-known American corporations as Disney World, Greyhound Bus Lines, and Amtrak, to name a few. With a second office in Alexandria, Virginia, serving the megalopolis of Fairfax County, Virginia, Prince George's County, Maryland, and the city of Washington, D.C., American Uniform Sales, Inc., is a Fayetteville success story.

One will find no more vocal advocate for Fayetteville than Rajan Shamdasani, president of American Uniform Sales, Inc. A native of India, Shamdasani was educated in Hong Kong and has traveled the world extensively. It is a tribute to Fayetteville that the Shamdasani family has chosen the city as the setting in which to pursue its progressive and successful business ventures.

In 1987, the Shamdasani family decided to diversify its business holdings. Twenty-two acres of land near Fayetteville's Sycamore Dairy Road, linking busy Bragg Boulevard with the rapidly growing area near Cross Creek Mall, was purchased. In an amazingly short time, the area was transformed into the Omni Plaza complex, which includes office buildings, movie theaters, miniature golf, and other recreational businesses. Later, a tract of land was purchased on Bragg Boulevard, and ambitious plans are being drawn up for that site's development.

When Fayetteville experienced a building boom following the end of the Gulf War in the early 1990s, the Shamdasani family entered the field of residential construction, with two of its projects being the Galleria Condominiums and the Pebble Creek subdivision. A 350-unit, single-family subdivision is being planned for nearby Hope Mills.

Refocusing energy on the uniform sales business in the mid-1990s, American Uniform Sales has acquired a factory in Puerto Rico and is enjoying record sales.

The entire Shamdasani family is aware of its responsibilities to the community. Members of the family serve on various civic boards and professional associations and are known to be generous contributors to such community groups as the public schools and other civic organizations.

The success of the Shamdasani family and its various business enterprises lends credence to the identity Fayetteville enjoys as a cosmopolitan city, full of economic opportunity.

"This is a family business," says Rajan Shamdasani, pointing out that his brothers, Ashok and Deepak, and his sister, Kathy, are an integral part of the operation. "All of us derive our motivation from our parents, who still are the beacon of light most families seek."

Shamdasani family

There may well be no nonprofit organization that is more supportive of Faytteville's community activities than the Veterans of Foreign Wars Post 6018, named in honor of the late James B. Dennis, one of the post's founding members.

The 850-member post, more than 600 of them life members, make up the fifth largest VFW post in North Carolina. Among the membership are veterans of World War II, as well as subsequent conflicts, and at least two women, veterans of the Army's Nurse Corps. Every rank under that of general officer is represented among the post's membership. An auxiliary unit of the spouses, daughters, and sisters of active VFW members maintains a membership of more than 300, and they are a driving force within the post.

room, a membership lounge, a kitchen, and office space. Here, the members enjoy fellowship with one another and participate actively in the community.

The activities undertaken by the members of VFW Post 6018 and its auxiliary are too numerous to list; however, there is no day in which a member of the post is not represented among the volunteers at the local Veterans Affairs Hospital. The post is a Partner in Education with Walker-Spivey School, hosting parties and providing special attention for the exceptional children who attend it. The post provides support for other schools in the system as well and is the only VFW post to offer in-house tutoring for elementary school children. The post offers scholarships annually, as well as financial assistance to youngsters who need it to participate in extra-curricular activities.

Many community agencies have turned to VFW Post 6018 for assistance in delivering Christmas treats to the needy, or window fans to those in need of them, or for any number of other helpful undertakings.

The post has received numerous state and national VFW awards for its community services. In 1995, the post placed first among VFW posts in the state for community service activities and fifth among the 10,000-plus VFW posts in the nation.

Providing a valuable civic service to its members and others in the community, the post sponsors periodic candidate forums, inviting candidates for public office

Established in 1970 with 51 members, the James B. Dennis VFW Post 6018 has flourished. In 1993, the organization moved from cramped quarters into a spacious 9,000-square-foot building near Fayetteville's city center, at 116 Chance Street, the culmination of a $500,000 project. The building includes an attractive lobby, a large meeting

into the post for enlightening question and answer sessions with the membership.

A recent past commander of the post, Charles Cole, says the VFW motto is "Honor the Dead by Helping the Living." The James B. Dennis VFW Post 6018 has certainly imbued that motto with real meaning for Fayetteville, North Carolina.

MARVIN ALLAN DOOR COMPANY, INC.

White work trucks emblazoned with the name Marvin Allan Door Company are an increasingly familiar sight on the streets of Fayetteville. The company is a successful beneficiary of the building boom that has occurred in the city in the past decade. An increased demand for new homes translates directly into an increased demand for the high-quality garage doors and garage door openers that are the mainstay of Marvin Allan Door.

Marvin Allan, the firm's founder, started the business in the early 1980s as he was making the transition into the civilian world after a long career in the military. Allan smilingly says he started out "with a pickup truck and a little bit of luck." Initially a home improvement company, the firm developed its current specialty as the demand for safe, high-quality garage doors and openers increased dramatically.

In addition to constructing new doors, the company replaces aging or damaged doors on existing homes. Marvin Allan Door Company is a 24-hour-a-day, seven-day-a-week business that prides itself on its quick response to customers' calls.

For the customer who has the skills to do an installation or repair without help, Marvin Allan Door Company offers its products at retail. The firm features Wayne Dalton doors and openers manufactured by Chamberlain, the world's largest producer of garage door openers.

From the perspective of hard-earned success, Marvin says he is eager to give back to the community that has sustained his business. The company, which now employs about 16 people, is a member of the Fayetteville Area Home Builders Association, the Fayetteville Chamber of Commerce, and the Fayetteville Area Economic Development Corporation. An active participant in the work of each of these organizations, Allan believes the Fayetteville area has a bright economic future. He bases that belief on the continued presence and importance of the military complex at Fort Bragg and Pope Air Force Base as well as on the other growth and development occurring in the region.

"I think Fayetteville will continue to experience growth for the foreseeable future," Allan says.

RATLEY CONSTRUCTION COMPANY, INC.

Drive down almost any street in Fayetteville and you will see evidence of the work of Ratley Construction Company. From the neighborhood Quick Stop to the newest McDonald's, Ratley Construction Company has been an important participant in the growth and economic development of Fayetteville, offering its services to a list of major corporations, including NationsBank, Advance Auto, Jiffy Lube, and BB&T.

Ratley Construction Company is proud to call Fayetteville home. Dan Ratley, the company's founder, is a loyal fan of the area. "With the potential that existed in Fayetteville in 1975, the military presence, and the ideal geographical location that it enjoys," Ratley says, "I knew it would be a good area to establish a business." Ratley Construction Company is a charter member of the Fayetteville Area Economic Development Corporation, a supporter of the Fayetteville YMCA, and a member of the Fayetteville Chamber of Commerce.

As Fayetteville has grown, so has Ratley Construction Company. Beginning as a residential builder in 1975, the company has maintained the same philosophy throughout the years: to offer high-quality construction at a fair price with an emphasis on customer satisfaction. Completing its first commercial building in 1979, Ratley Construction Company went on to build restaurants, shopping centers, office complexes, medical facilities, educational institutions, and many other commercial buildings for firms across the United States. Ratley's reputation for delivering on time and within budget makes it easy to understand why these clients have become repeat customers.

Ratley Construction Company has become an industry leader in commercial construction in the Southeast. Offering single-source accountability, Ratley Construction Company can offer its clients professional assistance in everything from site selection to occupancy of a first-class building. This has led to significant growth for the company, which is now licensed in 10 states, Puerto Rico, and the Virgin Islands. The company maintains offices in Pompano Beach, Florida, and Rio Piedras, Puerto Rico, as well as its local main office.

Just as Fayetteville looks forward to a bright future, Ratley Construction Company looks forward to continuing to be an active partner in the place it calls home.

BUTLER'S ELECTRIC SUPPLY OF FAYETTEVILLE

The history of Butler's Electric Supply of Fayetteville dates back to 1954, six years after the company was established in Whiteville by James P. Butler. The Fayetteville store is still a family-owned company, managed by John Butler, and his three brothers and a cousin manage stores in Wilmington, High Point, and Pinehurst, North Carolina, and Myrtle Beach, South Carolina.

Customer satisfaction, in all aspects of the business, is the main mission in the company.

"We are a service-oriented company," says John Butler, "and we provide our customers with the best possible service."

Butler's Electric Supply of Fayetteville, located at 1500 Ramsey Street, is much more than a supplier of such utilitarian items as electrical wire or breaker panels. The firm also sells lighting fixtures, chandeliers, and lamps, as well as decorative accessories such as oil paintings, prints, mirrors, and occasional furniture pieces. Walking into the showroom, one is struck by the unique wares and the dazzling array of sparkling chandeliers and fixtures. The helpful sales staff who greet customers are happy to assist in the selection of just the right lamp to complement a certain decor, or with much simpler tasks, such as finding the right light bulb for a distinctive fixture.

Butler's Electric Supply represents approximately 50 fixture manufacturers, 150 supply companies, and 15 or 20 accessory suppliers. With such a selection to offer its customers, Butler's usually has what a customer needs, or the means to locate it.

John Butler points out that although the beautiful showroom is an important aspect of the company, a substantial percentage of the firm's business is in electrical supplies used in the strong building boom that continues in the Fayetteville area.

Butler's Electric Supply is an active participant in the business community in Fayetteville, maintains memberships in the Fayetteville Home Builders Association, the Fayetteville Chamber of Commerce, and the local Braxton Bragg chapter of the Association of the United States Army.

Butler's Electric Supply can be expected to continue illuminating homes and businesses throughout Fayetteville and the surrounding area. This successful company is a part of a thriving business community that is making Fayetteville's future such a bright one.

The long and distinguished history of Highsmith-Rainey Memorial Hospital is closely linked with the history of a developing Fayetteville. Almost a century ago, in 1901, Dr. Jacob Franklin Highsmith established the first private hospital in the state. With the subsequent help of Dr. William Thomas Rainey, the hospital, which was located near the top of Haymount Hill, grew to become one of the leading medical facilities in the region. The site of the former Highsmith-Rainey Hospital is now Cumberland County Mental Health Center.

In the early 1980s, construction began on the new Highsmith-Rainey Memorial Hospital on the corner of Ray and Robeson streets, marking some of the first revitalization of the downtown area. Hospital Corporation of America (HCA), based in Nashville, Tennessee, purchased the hospital and was proud to open the brand new, 150-bed facility in 1983. Within two years, HCA also built the Medical Arts Building, which now houses many physicians' offices, a diagnostic center, a magnetic resonance imaging center, and other business operations of the hospital.

In February 1994, HCA and Columbia Healthcare Corporation, based in Louisville, Kentucky, merged, forming the largest healthcare services provider in the nation. Since then, the companies have merged with several other providers, including HealthTrust. Highsmith-Rainey is proud to be part of this corporation, which currently operates more than 300 hospitals and 125 surgery centers and employs 190,000 professionals across the country.

In the years since the opening of the new facility, Highsmith-Rainey Memorial Hospital has prospered, providing excellent medical care to its patients.

With encouragement and support from the corporate office, Highsmith-Rainey became the first healthcare provider in the community to implement a quality improvement program, which was started in 1989. The mission and vision for Highsmith-Rainey and all the former HCA hospitals was to establish quality guidelines for every customer. As healthcare issues change and evolve, so too will the hospital's vision, but the mission remains constant:

- *To provide excellence in healthcare;*
- *To improve the standards of healthcare in our community;*
- *To provide quality facilities and services to enable physicians to best serve the needs of our patients;*
- *To generate measurable benefits for:*
  The Community
  The Employee
  The Medical Staff and, most importantly,
  The Patient

So enduring is this mission statement that it is engraved on bronze plaques on each floor of the hospital, a perpetual reminder to the healthcare professionals and a reassurance to those who are acknowledged to be their most important consideration, the patient.

Highsmith-Rainey is proud to offer a variety of services to the community, including emergency care, ambulatory and inpatient surgery, intensive care/critical care units, general medical care, pediatrics, and, most recently, an obstetrics unit.

In the fall of 1995, the hospital opened the doors of its special delivery unit, which includes six labor, delivery, recovery, and postpartum suites and six overflow suites. Included in each suite is a bed, a bathroom with a Jacuzzi tub, a mini-refrigerator, a television and VCR, a sleeper sofa, a glider rocker, and an equipment closet that holds the bassinet and other equipment needed for the delivery. The overflow postpartum rooms and a surgery suite for cesarean section deliveries are just down the hall.

The staff in the special delivery unit pays extra attention to family and child, providing what is known at "couplet care," in which one nurse per shift is assigned to take care of mother and baby during the important initial bonding period.

As Highsmith-Rainey Memorial Hospital approaches the centennial anniversary of its establishment, it will continue to be an important part of the Fayetteville landscape, providing choice and excellence in medical care to the region's residents.

The administration and staff of Highsmith-Rainey are proud to be part of the downtown Fayetteville area and look forward to future construction projects as they expand their medical campus by providing, among other services, office space for physicians recruited to meet the needs of the growing Cumberland County community.

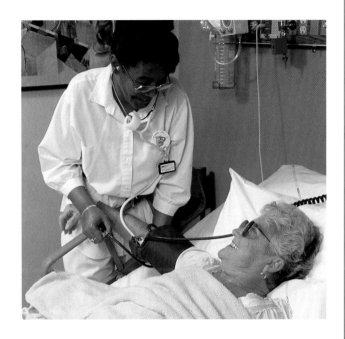

© Cramer Gallimore

American Carpets and Interiors, established in 1966, is a remarkable success story, both for Fayetteville and for the company's founder, Harold Brewington.

A dynamic and hard-charging man, Brewington has built his company, which was originally American Tile and Flooring Service, into a multidivisional company whose combined annual sales, in the mid-1990s, exceeded $13 million.

Employing more than 125 people among four divisions—American Carpets and Interiors, American Ceramic Tile Distributors, American Designer Rugs, and American Carpet Care—the

firm now has outlets in Fayetteville, Pinehurst, and Wilmington. Having evolved into a true interior design business, American Carpets and Interiors can provide customers with carpeting, window treatments, tiling, and handmade Oriental rugs. A recent affiliation with Carpetmax, the largest carpet service group in the nation, enables American Carpets and Interiors to offer its customers the best selection and prices in the country, a edge that can't be matched by the company's competitors.

The American Carpets and Interiors Fayetteville showroom is a busy place, humming with activity as sales staff and customers, surrounded by carpet samples and fabric swatches, ponder and compare the various options in interior decor.

Harold Brewington attributes his company's success to a commitment to an adherence to the fundamental principles of honesty and integrity. It's a commitment that all employees of American Carpets and Interiors share, along with an equal commitment to customer satisfaction,

Much of American Carpets and Interiors' customer base is made up of repeat customers, from individuals to national corporations, that have learned over the years that there is no better company than American Carpets and Interiors to assist with their flooring needs.

Concerned about the level of professional expertise throughout the industry, Harold Brewington has been a moving force in establishing standards and a course of instruction for future flooring installers. Believing that meaningful careers can be found in the floor-covering industry, Brewington helped develop a pilot program in the school system to teach high school students the skills necessary to embark on such a career.

American Carpets and Interiors is a member of the Chamber of Commerce, and Brewington is an enthusiastic member of the Chamber's Military Affairs Council. The company is also a member of the North Carolina Flooring Association.

As a business that understands the concept of excellence, American Carpets and Interiors is an important presence in Fayetteville's business community.

Harold Brewington

The Fayetteville Museum of Art has been a presence in Fayetteville's cultural life since 1971. Each year, the museum presents as many as 10 art exhibitions at its handsome gallery, the first building in the state designed and constructed as an art museum. In addition, traveling exhibitions of national and international importance are featured and remain on view for an average of six to eight weeks. The museum also serves as the setting for concerts and other cultural events throughout the year.

The Fayetteville Museum of Art is the site for an annual competition for North Carolina artists and a concurrent exhibition, which has earned a reputation for being one of the Southeast's most distinguished and professionally juried annual shows.

Educating the general public about art at a variety of levels is one of the museum's priorities. An ongoing program of films and lectures about art-related subjects is presented in the lecture hall on the lower level of the museum. Art classes, for adults and children, are also given on the lower level throughout the year.

To illuminate the subject of art for schoolchildren, the museum offers conducted tours of the galleries, led by trained volunteer docents, in a program known as "I'm a Good Looker." Bringing more than 6,000 schoolchildren to the museum annually, the program does a great deal to promote understanding and appreciation of art.

The museum maintains a permanent collection of more than 300 works of art, primarily by contemporary North Carolina artists. Pieces of sculpture grace the museum's 5.6 acres of landscaped grounds. In addition, the museum counts among its collection more than 75 artifacts from the Helen Smith Moore Collection of African Art, collected in the 1920s and 1940s from Liberia, as well as more than 150 rare artifacts from the Lewis Pate Collection of African Art, from Mali and Zaire.

Tom Grubb, the museum's director, serves as a member of the Business for Arts and Culture Committee of the Fayetteville Chamber of Commerce. The staff of the Fayetteville Museum of Art know that the museum is an important part of Fayetteville's quality of life and support the ongoing efforts to enhance the livability of the city.

As Fayetteville and the surrounding 10-county region grow and develop, the Fayetteville Museum of Art will continue to serve as a regional center for the arts, playing a major role in the area's exciting cultural life.

RAMADA INN

Fayetteville's only Ramada Inn is conveniently located on one of the city's busiest thorough-fares, near the airport, the Cumberland County Civic Center, and downtown Fayetteville.

Purchased by the DJP Corporation in 1994, the Ramada Inn subsequently underwent a complete renovation. From the spacious lobby to each of the 137 rooms, the decor and appointments were updated, imbuing the hotel with a gracious and contemporary ambience. Among the amenities the hotel now offers are courtesy van service to the airport, a private swimming pool, satellite television, banquet and meeting facilities, and the Sutter Street Restaurant and Lounge.

The Ramada Inn is proud of its high occupancy rate and is often completely booked on summer weekends. The hotel's guests, who represent a diverse clientele, can range from military officers in town for temporary duty at Fort Bragg or Pope Air Force Base to the Interstate 95 traveler who wants to stop at the midway point between New York and Disney World. The hotel also hosts a number of bus tours and offers golf packages that attract many guests.

Sutter Street Restaurant and Lounge offers tasty food to the hotel's visitors, as well as to residents of Fayetteville who know good food when they find it. From a full breakfast menu to a fine dinner of prime rib, Sutter Street Restaurant and Lounge can provide just the right meal. Thursday and Friday nights are the busiest, since that's when the after-work crowd gathers to listen to the sounds of karaoke in the inviting and relaxing atmosphere of the lounge.

The Ramada Inn is the setting for many meetings and wedding receptions in Fayetteville. The hotel's banquet room accommodates as many as 200 guests.

The Ramada Inn is an active member of the Fayetteville Area Hospitality Association and the Fayetteville Chamber of Commerce. As a representative of the hospitality industry, the Ramada Inn will be making a positive impression on visitors to Fayetteville for some time to come.

Cumberland Community Foundation

The Cumberland Community Foundation was established in 1980 through the vision and generosity of the late Dr. Lucile Hutaff to serve Fayetteville and the surrounding region. Its primary goal is to improve the quality of life for all citizens in the community now and in the future. It accomplishes this goal by securing permanent charitable dollars, investing them wisely, and distributing the income to meet ever-changing community needs.

To carry out its work, the Foundation enters into two kinds of partnerships, one with caring donors who provide the resources and the other with organizations capable of implementing the programs required. The Cumberland Community Foundation offers many ways for donors to participate, serving equally well those of modest means or substantial wealth. All know the Foundation preserves their gift and respects their initial intent forever. The Foundation can tailor funds to accommodate specific giving interests of donors. Alternatively, donors may request that their contribution be put in the Foundation's general purpose endowment to provide flexible revenue.

A single gift, regardless of its size, can make a remarkable difference in many lives for generations to come. The gift keeps on giving! The impact of this young and vibrant community foundation has already been felt by children and adults alike through hundreds of grant awards in the fields of the arts, culture, education, the environment, human services, and recreation.

The Foundation is managed by a professional staff and governed by a local board of directors representing diverse experiences and perspectives. They offer prudent stewardship of resources and encourage innovative solutions to local challenges.

The Cumberland Community Foundation is an important part of Fayetteville's rapid rise from small town to big city, providing a conduit for capital that fuels progress and positive change. It is also a thoughtful arena in which community initiatives can be proposed, evaluated, and prioritized.

The Foundation strives to preserve the legacy of its founder and to encourage participation from everyone willing to act for the good of the community. This goal is summed up in the words of the current executive director, Aline R. Lambert: "Since 1980, we have been the bridge between those who want their contributions to be permanent and the rest of the community."

Aline R. Lambert, executive director of the Cumberland Community Foundation, in front of its center on Green Street

OLDE FAYETTEVILLE ASSOCIATION

The Olde Fayetteville Association is an organization that is devoted to the development of Fayetteville's downtown as the "heart" of the community. The association's vision of a vibrant city center includes business development as well as cultural activities that will draw people to the nucleus of Fayetteville.

The Olde Fayetteville Association is coordinating a community-wide effort called "A Complete Fayetteville, Once and for All." This initiative has retained the nationally known and highly respected talents and vision of architect Robert Marvin, who has designed and built some of the most beautiful areas in the South. Input from a cross-section of local citizens on how Fayetteville's downtown can become architecturally unique and culturally appealing is also a part of the planning process.

Made up of more than 200 members, the association includes interested businesses and individuals who live and work throughout Fayetteville. The common denominator among them is the belief that Fayetteville's historically rich downtown has great potential and that meeting that potential will benefit the entire community.

Established in 1963 as the Downtown Fayetteville Association, then merging with Fayetteville Progress, the Olde Fayetteville Association has evolved from being primarily a coalition of downtown merchants to having a business development focus and a strong concentration on the arts.

The association works closely with city and county governments. The sharing of ideas and information among these government bodies and other organizations is of great benefit to the association in promoting the cultural aspects of the city center. Olde Fayetteville hosts five events annually that draw more than 100,000 people to the area and attract every segment of the population. In its seventeenth year, the International Folk Festival, at which more than 30 countries are represented, celebrates Fayetteville's cultural diversity.

The Olde Fayetteville Association is a progressive partner with those who work for Fayetteville's bright future, one that will include a healthy "start" for the city.

POWERS-SWAIN CHEVROLET-GEO

The Powers-Swain Chevrolet-Geo dealership has been a part of the Fayetteville business scene for more than 35 years. Founded in 1961 by C. C. Powers, Jr., and his brothers-in-law, E. L. and Sigmund Swain, at a time when Dinah Shore was inviting drivers to "see the USA in a Chevrolet," the company has grown and flourished in the intervening decades.

C. C. Powers, Jr., died unexpectedly in 1984, presenting the company with a dilemma. Ownership of the company had been transferred to Powers as he bought out the interests of the Swain brothers over the years. Upon his death, his wife, Peggy Powers, who had long been a homemaker and mother, was faced with the decision of whether to sell the company or assume the leadership responsibilities of dealer/operator. Rising gracefully to the occasion, Peggy Powers led the company for more than a decade, always encouraging her staff to provide the same level of service to customers that they would want for themselves.

General Manager W. C. Powers is the son of the late C. C. Powers, Jr. A dentist by profession, the younger Powers has gradually assumed the leadership of the company. He is quick to point out that the loyalty and devotion of the company's employees, many of whom have been with the firm for more than 25 years, are among the important reasons the company has succeeded for so long.

One of the measures of that success is the World Class rating Powers-Swain consistently earns from General Motors. Based on a number of criteria related to customer satisfaction, a dealership must sustain a 90 percent achievement level to be awarded the World Class rating. That designation is meaningful to Powers-Swain employees—they all believe that customer satisfaction is an absolute imperative.

The company is an active corporate citizen and a strong supporter of Fort Bragg and Pope Air Force Base. With a sincere interest in the continued growth and development of Fayetteville as a business and cultural center for the region, Powers-

Swain actively participates in the Fayetteville Chamber of Commerce and the Chamber's Military Affairs Council, as well as in local chapters of the Air Force Association and the Association of the United States Army.

Powers-Swain and Fayetteville share decades of fascinating history. Together, the city and the company will move into the new century with an optimistic view that the future for each will be even brighter.

iversification is not just a buzzword at Weaver Development Company, Inc. Established in 1980 by E. Frank Weaver III to manage various business interests, the company now includes land development and construction operations. Further diversification spawned three related companies serving all aspects of real estate in Fayetteville and the surrounding area.

Weaver Commercial Properties was established in 1985 to acquire, sell, lease, and manage commercial land and buildings; Weaver Residential Real Estate, established in 1988, now CENTURY 21 Weaver-Fulghum, markets new and existing homes and manages residential properties; and Crown General Contractors, established in 1993 and based in Raleigh, is a design/build commercial construction business. These four companies, each focused on a different aspect of the real estate market but working together, in combination represent a full-service real estate firm serving the mid-Atlantic region.

Weaver's management team offers its customers and clients more than 100 years of combined experience in the real estate field. A commitment to excellence is a prerequisite to joining the Weaver team, and it is a commitment that never wavers.

Frank Weaver, founder and president, says, "We take great pride in our growing list of satisfied clients and customers, and we look forward with great anticipation as Fayetteville continues its remarkable growth and development."

The leaders of the companies affiliated with Weaver Development Company, Inc.: (seated left to right) Janice Cox, project coordinator, Crown General Contractors, Inc.; Frank Weaver; Helga Ochoa, comptroller for all companies; (standing left to right) John Bantsolas, property manager and broker, Weaver Commercial Properties; Bob Mitchell, general manager, Crown General Contractors, Inc.; Dan Hall, commercial project manager, Weaver Development Company, Inc.; Tony Weaver, vice president and general manager, Weaver Development Company, Inc.; Joe Price, residential project coordinator, Weaver Development Company, Inc. Not pictured: Gerald Fulghum, manager/broker, CENTURY 21 Weaver-Fulghum; Kathleen Vergan, accounting for all companies.

YARBOROUGH AND HANCOX, ATTORNEYS AT LAW

The law firm of Yarborough and Hancox combines the talents and experience of two well-established and respected Fayetteville attorneys, Garris Neil Yarborough and Bradford Scott Hancox, to provide big-city legal services with a hometown touch. Working in different practice areas, with assistance from their associate, Chris Salyer, and a competent support staff, the firm provides a broad array of legal services to local, regional, and national clients.

Neil Yarborough has an extensive record of public service. He currently serves as the county attorney for Cumberland and Hoke counties and as the town attorney for St. Pauls in Robeson County. In addition to municipal law, Yarborough concentrates his practice on the areas of construction, corporate, and real estate law. An experienced trial attorney, Yarborough received his law degree from the University of North Carolina in 1977 and a master's degree from Duke University the same year.

Scott Hancox, a former assistant district attorney in Fayetteville, concentrates on the areas of personal injury litigation, wills, estates, and general trial work. Representative of Fayetteville's multilingual population, Hancox is fluent in French, having lived in France, Africa, and the Caribbean as the son of a missionary. A graduate of the University of Tennessee and the Campbell University School of Law, Hancox has practiced law in the Fayetteville area since 1987 and is court-certified as a mediator.

Chris Salyer, a 1993 graduate of Campbell University School of Law, assists Yarborough and Hancox in their trial work and is directly involved in the firm's collections and traffic court practice. Salyer is a Fayetteville native and a graduate of the University of North Carolina-Chapel Hill, where he earned his undergraduate degree in industrial relations.

Left to right: Bradford Scott Hancox, Garris Neil Yarborough, and Christopher T. Salyer

A business-oriented firm, Yarborough and Hancox represents national and local corporations as well as individuals in areas ranging from multimillion dollar commercial transactions to residential loan closings. The philosophy of the firm mandates excellent legal representation and professional service to all its clients, regardless of how complex or simple their needs may be.

The law firm of Yarborough and Hancox is housed in an attractive new building near the Cumberland County Court House. Involved in growth and development of the entire region of which Fayetteville is becoming a business and cultural center, the firm is positioned to be a key player in Fayetteville's bright future.

HOME FEDERAL SAVINGS AND LOAN ASSOCIATION

With its track record of providing its customers with stability, security, and sound financial decisions for more than 80 years, Home Federal Savings and Loan Association is one of Fayetteville's oldest financial institutions.

Home Federal's long history has been punctuated by challenges from both man and nature. Not only has the firm survived natural disasters, such as floods and hurricanes, and helped people recover financially from the effects of those storms, it has also survived manmade turbulence, such as the crash of 1929 and, decades later, the financially volatile 1980s, when so many less solid savings and loan institutions collapsed.

By virtue of its strong financial position, Home Federal has had a tremendous impact on Fayetteville's growth and development. Home Federal has made the American dream of home ownership possible for many Fayettevillians and has created countless jobs while simultaneously providing solid stable investment opportunities for its savings customers.

Much of Home Federal's stability can be credited to the local community leaders who have served as directors of the institution over the years. There are 37 names on that distinguished list, all of whom were or are successful business professionals. Their careful stewardship of Home Federal's assets and their ability to chart a careful course for investment have earned Home Federal the fine reputation it enjoys today.

Home Federal Savings and Loan Association maintains two convenient locations in Fayetteville, as well as an office in nearby Lumberton. The firm is a member of the Federal Deposit Insurance Corporation.

A conscientious corporate citizen, Home Federal maintains memberships in the Fayetteville Area Economic Development Corporation and the Fayetteville Chamber of Commerce. By supporting the efforts of these organizations to strengthen the local economy and provide a healthy economic climate, Home Federal is affirming its confidence in Fayetteville's bright future.

Home Federal's board of directors: (seated left to right) Henry Holt; Henry Hutaff; H. D. Reaves, Jr.; R. O. McCoy, Jr.; (standing left to right) Joe Hollinshed; John Pate; Norwood E. Bryan, Jr.; Robert G. Ray; and John Grantham

ts commitment to representing every client's interests effectively while maintaining an abiding interest in the business community at large is what makes
Hutchens & Senter such a well-respected law firm.

The firm does most of its work in business and
corporate law, although Hutchens & Senter offers
legal support in other areas of the law as well.
Concentrating on the legal aspects of incorporation,
real estate law, and contracts and business litigation,
Hutchens & Senter has established a reputation for
excellence that extends far beyond Fayetteville. A
glance at the firm's client roster indicates that many
well-known financial institutions from across the
state and region have chosen to have the firm provide
them with legal representation.

Located in one of Fayetteville's premier corporate
complexes, the United Carolina Bank Plaza,
Hutchens & Senter has an experienced and energetic
corps of attorneys and a highly trained and dedicated support staff.

The business community has reason to trust that
the firm will provide excellent service. Both the firm's

partners, H. Terry Hutchens and William Senter, are
highly visible in the local business community, as well
as in statewide organizations. Terry Hutchens has
served in several high-level leadership capacities with
the Fayetteville Chamber of Commerce and as a
board member of the North Carolina Department of
Transportation. He is also highly regarded nationally
within the ranks of the Republican Party. His well-
appointed office includes photographs of him with
three presidents as well as with the late chair of the
Republican Party, Lee Atwater.

William Senter served several years as chair of the
local Morehead Scholarship Committee. A
Morehead Scholar himself, he is committed to perpetuating the excellence fostered by the prestigious
scholarship and the bright young people who are its
beneficiaries.

Measuring the firm's success by the success of its
clients, Hutchens & Senter is confident about its
corporate future. The firm is certain to contribute to
Fayetteville's increasing importance as a business and
cultural center in the coming millennium.

H. Terry Hutchens and William Senter with their employees

Sprint/Carolina Telephone

print/Carolina Telephone has a tradition of growth and progress in eastern North Carolina In 1895, G. A. Holderness joined with several local businessmen to raise $2,500 and build a telephone company in Tarboro, North Carolina. They persuaded nine other Tarboro citizens to buy stock, and the Tarboro Telephone Company was born.

Starting with 30 customers, Holderness and his associates expanded into Washington, Kinston, and Fayetteville. The business, which became Carolina Telephone and Telegraph Company in 1900, has prospered ever since.

The company has always been a telecommunications pioneer in the state, whether it was making direct distance dialing available for the first time or introducing a microwave system between Fayetteville and Rocky Mount in 1957.

With more than 920,000 customer telephone lines in 50 of North Carolina's 100 counties, Sprint/Carolina Telephone's 100 percent digital network transmits volumes of data and precise voice communications statewide. The company's participation in such projects as the North Carolina Information Highway has helped make the state a national leader in communications technology.

In the Fayetteville area, Sprint/Carolina Telephone is helping Fayetteville State University and Fayetteville Technical Community College access the state's information highway and plans to continue adding sites.

In March 1993, Sprint Carolina Telephone began connecting the 112 barracks at Fort Bragg to the Mallonee central office using fiber-optic technology. Coined the fiber-in-the-loop (FITL) project, it is connecting more than 4,300 lines in the barracks.

The FITL project uses fiber-optic cable instead of copper wire so as to provide better quality telephone service and an easier-to-maintain system. The Fort Bragg network is the largest FITL project of its kind.

Sprint/Carolina Telephone is one of four Sprint companies in the Mid-Atlantic region that are providing local telecommunications products and services. The other companies are in South Carolina, Tennessee, and Virginia. Sprint is the country's only major company that provides long-distance, cellular, and local exchange service.

CUTLER-HAMMER

utler-Hammer is a world-class manufacturer of motor control assemblies. Using complex and sophisticated electronics equipment, the assemblies are mounted and wired into steel enclosures that ultimately are used to control motors and other electrical devices, safely and efficiently. The assemblies are found in a variety of industrial settings, including textile mills and paper mills, as well as other businesses.

Cutler-Hammer opened its plant in Fayetteville in 1980. Located on a 56-acre site near the airport, the plant includes 189,000 square feet of manufacturing space and an additional 36,000 square feet for offices. The plant has been expanded twice, in 1982 and again in 1984. In 1994, the company was acquired by the Eaton Corporation in its purchase of the Westinghouse Distribution and Control Business Unit.

Cutler-Hammer employs more than 700 people in Fayetteville and is recognized as a leader in the just-in-time (JIT) manufacturing process. JIT is a way to maximize the ability to fill orders quickly and efficiently for customers all over the world, while minimizing the need to maintain a large inventory.

The plant was awarded the ISO 9002 Award in 1994, reserved for companies that meet or exceed international quality standards.

Cutler-Hammer is a customer-driven operation, where teams of employees plan, schedule, and direct their own work, always with an unflagging commitment to meet customers' needs.

Involvement in the greater Fayetteville community is important to Cutler-Hammer, which is supportive of initiatives that affect the quality of life in Fayetteville. Not only is the company active in the business community as a member of the Fayetteville Chamber of Commerce and as a supporter of the Junior Achievement program, but Cutler-Hammer is also a significant contributor to the United Way of Cumberland County and a supporter of the March of Dimes Walk America campaign.

Cutler-Hammer is a company that puts Fayetteville on the global business map. With its commitment to total quality, Cutler-Hammer is competing internationally in a highly competitive environment. Proud of its reputation as an international competitor, Cutler-Hammer is also proud to be a part of Fayetteville's exciting future.

The LSV Partnership, the premier architectural firm in Fayetteville, has had a decided influence on the city's development. Throughout the city and the region, the firm's award-winning designs have taken various forms, from private residences and medical offices, to manufacturing facilities and showrooms, to public libraries and schools.

Among the most valued tributes the firm's work has earned are unsolicited testimony from clients:

Anyone who is lucky enough to have [The LSV Partnership] as the architects of a project will have a building that answers the practical needs of the client at the same time it makes a statement as to the eternal beauty and value of outstanding architectural design.

With the help of The LSV Partnership . . . the project came from conception to reality within six months—on time and within budget!

It was indeed a pleasure to work with you on the showroom, which is certainly one of, if not Noland's finest assets.

Walter Vick, the firm's principal architect, says that a client becomes part of the design process as the client and architect arrive at a complete and mutual understanding of the project's intended use.

"One doesn't sacrifice form to function," he says, "but form must function."

A full-service architectural and planning firm, The LSV Partnership also offers feasibility studies, economic analyses, site evaluations, and interior design services to its clients, which include national and regional corporations as well as local businesses and institutions.

The LSV Partnership's designs have won awards for architectural excellence not only from the architectural community in North Carolina but from the associations with which its clients are affiliated. For example, the North Carolina Library Directors Association awarded the Cliffdale Library its Best New Facility Award in 1991 and the Hope Mills Library the same award the next year.

The firm is a dedicated corporate citizen and a member of the Fayetteville Area Economic Development Corporation and the Fayetteville Chamber of Commerce. In 1994, the firm received the corporate award from the Fayetteville Minority Business Development Center for its support of and involvement with the minority business community.

As Fayetteville's future unfolds, The LSV Partnership, PA, Architects/Planners AIA, will be at the drawing board, helping make the city's best and brightest visions for the future come true.

PHP, INC.

Established in 1985 as Physicians Health Plan of North Carolina, Inc., and headquartered in Greensboro, North Carolina, PHP, Inc., is a health maintenance organization (HMO) that, since its start, has been committed to open access and consideration for the customer.

In addition to Fayetteville, PHP has offices in three other North Carolina cities: Asheville, Wilmington, and Cary.

Thousands of people in Fayetteville are enrolled in a PHP, Inc., plan and, like the overwhelming majority of PHP's 118,000-plus customers, most choose the open access model of coverage, enabling them to consult with any of PHP's 2,800 participating physicians without prior authorization.

PHP enjoys an extraordinary 96 percent satisfaction rate among its customers, according to a Gallup poll. The company is equally proud that Weiss Research gave PHP an A- financial rating, the highest such rating given to any managed health-care company in North Carolina.

PHP, Inc., was formed by a group of physicians who recognized in the early 1980s that changes in the delivery of health care were inevitable. Acknowledging that, they wanted to maintain the highest standards of medical care and patients' freedom to choose a physician. At the same time, they wanted to contain the soaring costs associated with every aspect of health care.

The company's first decade of success is reflected in its rapid, sustained growth. PHP contracts with more than 1,000 North Carolina employers, serving more than 118,000 individual customers. Preparing to serve an ever-growing customer base, PHP has developed a statewide network of more than 45 hospitals and 3,000 health-care providers. In addition, PHP maintains a network of pharmacies, physical therapists, and other allied health professionals.

In preparing for the twenty-first century, PHP recognizes that flexibility will be the imperative as it tries, proactively, to influence the process of delivering excellent health care to its customers. The company is committed to developing new managed-care products and partnerships in its quest to raise PHP's already high standards of service.

As Fayetteville moves toward its destiny as a regional business and cultural center, PHP, Inc., will be a presence in the city, a partner in Fayetteville's dynamic economic ascension and excellent quality of life.

HEALY WHOLESALE, INC.

ealy Wholesale, Inc., is a successful Fayetteville business that distributes and imports malt beverages and wines. The company's distinctive delivery vehicles are seen on highways and byways throughout the region, delivering beverages to area grocery stores, clubs, and restaurants.

Healy Wholesale made its debut on the Fayetteville business scene in 1978, when Frederick A. ("Fritz") Healy purchased the former Smithson Beverage Company. Over the years, subsequent acquisitions have extended the family-owned company's area of influence in North Carolina to 20 counties, from the Virginia border to the South Carolina line. Healy's main products are supplied by the Miller Brewing Company and the E & J Gallo Winery.

Fritz Healy, Sr., serves as the chairman of the company's board of directors. His elder son, John Macdonald ("Mac") Healy, is president, and younger son Frederick A. ("Fritz") Healy, Jr., is vice president. Their combined influence in Fayetteville's civic, cultural, and charitable initiatives is far too extensive to quantify and reflects the company's philosophy that a good business is one that gives back to the community that sustains it.

The average resident of the Fayetteville community, younger than the national average, represents the company's ideal customer. Many of these customers, who appreciate a particular malt beverage or seek out a special imported or domestic wine, are assigned to Fort Bragg or Pope Air Force Base.

A fervent proponent of the local military community, Fritz Healy, Sr., likens the presence of Fort Bragg and Pope AFB in Fayetteville to the beneficial effect of having another excellent university.

"Most of those people have lived all over the world," Healy says. But rather than merely acknowledging the benefit of the military presence, Healy Wholesale has made tangible contributions to perpetuating Fort Bragg and Pope AFB's continued presence. Fritz Healy, Sr., serves as chair of North Carolina Governor James B. Hunt, Jr.'s Military Affairs Commission and was instrumental in establishing the Airborne and Special Operations Museum Foundation, which is overseeing the construction of a world-class museum at Fort Bragg, scheduled to open in 1997.

Healy Wholesale, Inc., employing more than 100 people, is proud to be located in Fayetteville, North Carolina, and is optimistic about its future in a city that is rapidly becoming a regional center of business and culture.

A constituent institution of the University of North Carolina, Fayetteville State is one of the fastest-growing, most rapidly improving institutions of higher education in North Carolina. Student enrollment has increased by 56 percent in the past several years, and there has been a concurrent 30 percent increase in combined SAT scores.

FSU's 4,000 students benefit from personal interaction with a dedicated and professional faculty. Close to three-quarters of the full-time faculty hold terminal degrees in their fields, and classes average 20 students. This individual attention to academic achievement, combined with state-of-the-art computer and research facilities, ensure that FSU graduates are competitive in their fields. FSU boasts 12,000 alumni, many of whom have achieved distinction as educators, medical professionals, politicians, and business leaders.

Students may choose from 36 baccalaureate degree programs in the arts and sciences, education, and business. Fifteen master's degree programs are available, including the MBA. Fayetteville State also offers a doctoral degree in educational leadership. College transfer and associate's degree programs are available through FSU's Fort Bragg-Pope AFB Education Center.

More than 200 academically talented FSU students are awarded full scholarships from private sources each year, and financial aid is available. The total of federal, state, and private scholarships and financial aid awarded to students exceeds $6 million annually.

Conveniently located near the heart of Fayetteville, FSU's growing campus encompasses 42 buildings in an attractive mix of traditional and contemporary architecture. An investment of $9.5 million has recently been made in residence hall renovations, including air conditioning, structural improvements, and complete voice, cable, and data communications wiring. A $10.9 million health, physical education, and recreation building recently opened, and the student center will soon be expanded.

Founded in 1867 as the Howard School,

The Charles W. Chesnutt Library on the FSU campus

Fayetteville State University is proud of its distinction as the second-oldest public university in North Carolina. Serving all citizens of the region and state, the school is notable today as one of the most culturally diverse campus communities in North Carolina.

Physicians' Total Rehab is committed to being a leader in both rehabilitation and community service, making it a visible presence on the Fayetteville health-care scene.

As a physician-owned and operated comprehensive outpatient rehabilitation facility, Physicians' Total Rehab is premised on the belief that patients are provided the best possible rehabilitation opportunities when they are in their own homes, with friends and family to assist. Even those patients requiring intense, daily programs of therapy benefit from returning to

their own homes at the end of a day of rehabilitation services, which Physicians' Total Rehab provides at two locations, one on Village Drive in Fayetteville and one in Lumberton, North Carolina.

Total Rehab Orthotics and Prosthetics, Inc., is a separate but integral part of the Total Rehab system. The company provides state-of-the-art braces and artificial limbs, and the prosthetist, therapist, doctor, and patient all work together closely to get optimal results for the patient.

Those who benefit from a comprehensive outpatient rehabilitation facility include amputees and victims of strokes, severe arthritis, traumatic brain injuries, wounds, spinal cord injuries, work and sports injuries, and other medical problems. These patients retain the traditional physician-patient relationship, and their schedule of rehabilitation services can vary from daily to once a week. Physicians' Total Rehab maintains a fleet of three vehicles to transport patients at no charge.

In 1994, Physicians' Total Rehab established a charitable foundation to address health and wellness issues. The foundation has sponsored several worthy causes, including a special research project to help diabetics learn to manage their disease through exercise and a disabled swimmer who is pursuing a berth on the 1996 Paralympic Swimming Team. The foundation also organized a 15-member competition wheelchair basketball team and sponsors the largest wheelchair race in North Carolina.

Education is a focus of Physicians' Total Rehab, which throughout the year hosts seminars on health-related topics, publishes *Rehab Ramblings*, and serves as a training site for students from Fayetteville Technical Community College, Fayetteville Area Health Education Center, Fayetteville State University, and many other regional institutions.

As Fayetteville becomes the regional health-care center it is destined to be, Physicians' Total Rehab will continue to be a part of the city, providing a valuable service to thousands of the region's residents.

CTS Cleaning Systems, Inc.

CTS Cleaning Systems, Inc., is a family-owned business with a track record of almost three decades of providing companies in the Carolinas with industrial cleaning equipment, detergents, hydro-demolition, and waste water management systems.

CTS is proud of its status as the only cleaning equipment business on the East Coast to be certified by the Cleaning Equipment Trade Association. CTS is serious about offering the highest-quality products and service, environmental awareness, and technological development, along with a sincere desire to do what is right and best for its customers.

Fred R. Adkins established CTS Cleaning Systems, Inc., in 1967. In 1986, Rodney Adkins joined his father in the business of renting, leasing, selling, and maintaining pressure cleaning systems.

Both Fred and Rodney Adkins say their business is never routine. Each day brings a new challenge and new opportunities to serve their customers. One example of that is the company's involvement in the growing swine production industry in North Carolina. In 1990, CTS began manufacturing its own line of cold-water cleaning equipment to meet the needs of swine production. "Cleanliness of the hog houses is paramount in that industry," says Fred Adkins. "CTS has the equipment and the expertise to fill that need."

CTS Cleaning Systems has also assisted Fort Bragg, Pope AFB, New River Air Station, and the Marine Air Corps facility at Quantico, Virginia, with various unique tasks, including cleaning aircraft and a helicopter used by the president. Area marinas also consult CTS for specific cleaning applications and their potential environmental impact as well as treatment options.

The latest venture for CTS includes becoming the master distributor in North and South Carolina of a citrus-based cleaning product called Glowry.

CTS is a leader in furthering education in the cleaning equipment industry. Rodney Adkins serves on the board of directors of the Cleaning Equipment Trade Association and periodically writes for the industry's trade publication, Cleaner Times.

CTS Cleaning Systems, Inc., is a contributing cor-

Jeremy Ake, Karen Kollar, Fred Adkins, Rodney Adkins, and Bob Grunden

porate citizen in the Fayetteville community. A member of the Fayetteville Chamber of Commerce and the local Braxton-Bragg chapter of the Association of the U.S. Army, CTS also supports vocational education and contributes to numerous local charities.

CTS Cleaning Systems, Inc., is a part of the mosaic that is Fayetteville's growing business community. The company looks forward to Fayetteville's bright economic future, knowing that it is a part of that growth and development.

ADIA PERSONNEL SERVICES

The Adia Personnel Services office in Fayetteville is one of 1,200 such offices worldwide and is poised to help meet the growing demand for temporary employees, as well as permanent personnel, by the local business community.

According to Jim Caison, owner/manager of Adia Personnel Services in Fayetteville, the days are over when companies hired temporaries simply to fill in for employees who were sick or on vacation. As recruitment costs skyrocket, and as flexible working hours and lifestyles become more commonplace, many companies are making temporary help a line item on their budgets.

In a city like Fayetteville, where newcomers are arriving literally every day, Adia can provide access to the local workplace, which often leads to permanent employment. The name of the company (pronounced Ah-Dee´-Ah) is a familiar one to world travelers; founded in Lausanne, Switzerland, in 1957, Adia now has operations in 29 countries around the globe.

Adia in Fayetteville can provide personnel in nine general skill areas, including secretarial and clerical, light industrial, marketing, accounting, data processing, word processing, telemarketing, technical, and banking and financial services.

Conveniently located on Purdue Drive near Raeford Road, one of Fayetteville's busiest thoroughfares, the Adia office is staffed with business professionals and equipped with the latest in business technology.

In 1993, the Adia office in Fayetteville was designated the winner of the New Franchise of the Year Award by Adia's corporate headquarters in Redwood Shores, California. Adia is also a good corporate citizen; its owner/manager and the company's employees are involved in several community initiatives that are enhancing the quality of life in Fayetteville.

The staff at Adia are grateful to their clients and their workers for their support and strong and continuing partnership.

Fayetteville's dynamic business community is rapidly becoming the business and cultural center of the region. Adia Personnel Services will be a part of that bright future in Fayetteville, North Carolina.

Robyn Burris, Jim Caison, and Jackie Bunch

BRIGGS AND SONS TIRE

Briggs and Sons Tire, established in 1971 in Clinton, North Carolina, has been a presence on the Fayetteville business scene since 1987. The company is owned by Bob Briggs and his wife, Barbara. In 1971, the Briggses were a young married couple with a growing family. Now, two of their sons and a daughter-in-law are also active in the business.

An independent dealer for Goodyear, Briggs and Sons Tire has several locations in Fayetteville and Clinton. One of Goodyear's most successful dealerships, Briggs and Sons now employs 65 people and continues to expand. The company is testimony to the success that can be achieved when one combines hard work, the ability to recognize opportunity, a willingness to take risks, and unwavering optimism.

The company's immaculate white trucks, emblazoned with the blue-and-gold Goodyear logo, are now a familiar sight on Fayetteville's streets. Providing a variety of automotive services as well as tires and accessories, Briggs and Sons Tire is very comfortable with its identity as a service provider. As Barbara Briggs acknowledges, "We are a service-oriented business and we serve the public."

The Briggses were honored in 1993 with Methodist College's Silver Spoon Award, given annually to a person who has achieved business success on his or her own merits, without the advantages of wealth. The couple has also enjoyed incentive awards, usually in the form of luxurious trips, bestowed by the Goodyear Tire and Rubber Company for having met or exceeded sales goals. Yet the Briggses are not resting on their business laurels; even now, they can most often be found at work.

Briggs and Sons Tire shares its success with Fayetteville by sponsoring Little League teams or productions at the Cape Fear Regional Theater or by supporting the local professional team, the Fayetteville Generals. A member of the Fayetteville Chamber of Commerce, Briggs and Sons Tire is contributing to Fayetteville's healthy business climate and thereby helping other entrepreneurs to succeed as well.

Fayetteville is fortunate to be home to Briggs and Sons Tire, a business that embodies the best of the American entrepreneurial spirit.

ROGERS AND BREECE FUNERAL HOME

Rogers and Breece Funeral Home, established in 1898 by the late Oscar P. Breece, Sr., will soon embark on its second century of providing caring service to the people of Fayetteville.

A family-owned business since its inception, the company remains so. Robert W. Breece, Sr., serves as president, and his two sons, Robert W. Breece, Jr., and Corey R. Breece, are actively involved in the business.

The company provides traditional funeral services to its clients, including the use of the company's spacious and beautifully appointed funeral home and chapel.

Today, more and more people are arranging their own funerals; Rogers and Breece can offer them many options, including traditional burial, cremation, or memorial or graveside services. Rogers and Breece also cooperates with other funeral services across the country in arranging for a decedent's remains to be transported to or from Fayetteville.

With the motto "Our Family Serving Your Family," Rogers and Breece is well positioned to meet many of the needs that arise in planning a memorable funeral. The family's floral business, Breece Greenhouses, can arrange for floral arrangements appropriate for any funeral, from the simplest to the most elaborate.

The Breece family has established Fayetteville Memorial Cemetery and Mausoleums on a 78-acre site on Fayetteville's southern periphery and offers clients a variety of monuments, memorials, and mausoleum crypts in a range of prices.

A unique service offered by Rogers and Breece is the Tribute Program, which is a 16-minute video recording that includes as many as 15 photos of significant moments from the deceased's life, set to an appropriate musical accompaniment and interspersed with background scenes. An increasing number of people are choosing this program as a way to create a permanent record of a beloved's life, one that can be handed down to future generations.

The Breece family offers another service to the people of Fayetteville, one that stems from their desire to be a part of happy times as well as those occasions associated with loss and sadness. The Breece Limousine Service has a fleet of eight limousines, including a 120-inch stretch limo that accommodates 10 to 12 people and is outfitted with a bar, a color TV, and a stereo system. These limousines, complete with uniformed chauffeurs, transport Fayettevillians to proms, parties, concerts, anniversary celebrations, and many other festive occasions. Sometimes they are used to bring a new baby home from the hospital.

Rogers and Breece, with its long and distinguished history of service to Fayetteville's families, is equally proud of the continuing role the company will play in Fayetteville's future.

Robert W. Breece, Jr., Robert W. Breece, Sr., and Corey R. Breece

BRANCH BANKING AND TRUST

Branch Banking and Trust, better known in Fayetteville by its initials, BB&T, is the principal subsidiary of Southern National Corporation, a multibank holding company headquartered in Winston-Salem.

With 12 convenient locations throughout the metropolitan area, BB&T is a well-known presence in Fayetteville. It is the largest bank in the city by market share, with $350 million in deposits and $300 million in loans, and it employs more than 170 Fayetteville residents.

One discerns that BB&T is a unique corporate entity from the bank's mission statement:

To make the world a better place to live by
• Helping our customers achieve economic success and financial security;
• Creating a place where our employees can learn, grow, and be fulfilled in their work;
• Making the communities we serve a better place to be;
• Optimizing the long-term return to our shareholders while providing a safe and sound investment.

James ("Brownie") McLeod, BB&T's city executive in Fayetteville, says BB&T takes every component of that mission statement seriously.

"We focus on customers, employees, and communities," he says, "and the commitment to our shareholders is the bottom line."

McLeod notes that BB&T customers get help from the bank in maximizing the value of their money, employees are encouraged to seek upward mobility within the bank, and the communities served by BB&T are indeed made better by the bank's corporate involvement in a variety of community programs. All of this contributes to the bank's success, thus making it a sound investment for all the bank's shareholders.

Fayetteville's economic climate is important to BB&T. As a member of the Fayetteville Area Economic Development Corporation and the Fayetteville Chamber of Commerce, BB&T is visible among those who are working hardest to create an inviting quality of life and to recruit industry into the area.

BB&T is a Partner in Education with the Cumberland County School System, having taken District 7 Elementary School under its corporate wing. BB&T is also an extremely conscientious corporate citizen and is supportive of many civic and cultural initiatives in Fayetteville. The bank's influence is felt throughout the community.

Branch Banking & Trust will continue to be an important corporate contributor to the economic, civic, and cultural life of Fayetteville as the city moves toward the twenty-first century, with its new challenges and opportunities.

CAPE FEAR ORTHOPAEDIC CLINIC

ape Fear Orthopaedic Clinic is an association of orthopedic physicians, all of whom are board-certified. The practice, located on Medical Drive in Fayetteville, near Cape Fear Valley Medical Center, also employs several physician assistants as part of its commitment to serve patients effectively and efficiently.

Established in 1977, the Cape Fear Orthopaedic Clinic focuses exclusively on the diagnosis and treatment of orthopedic problems, with a special emphasis on sports medicine and arthroscopic knee surgery. One of the surgeons associated with the clinic is a specialist in hand injuries, including reconstructive surgery.

The Cape Fear Orthopaedic Clinic illustrates the close ties that exist between the military and civilian communities of Fayetteville. Three of the physicians associated with the clinic are veterans of the U.S. armed forces and were recalled to active duty during the Gulf War. The experience gained from treating the orthopedic injuries and diseases incurred by soldiers is invaluable in assessing similar conditions among the civilian population.

The medical professionals at Cape Fear Orthopaedic Clinic, in addition to being expert in their medical specialties, are committed to public health issues. They work each year with the North Carolina Medical Society Auxiliary Health Education Foundation on behalf of the organization's annual fund-raiser. One of the doctors has also appeared regularly on "Doctors on Call," a local call-in show on WKFT-TV. Several of the physicians serve as doctors for area high school football teams. And, ardent fans of the local professional baseball team, the Fayetteville Generals, the clinic's physicians provide medical attention to team members.

The clinic's physicians are also committed to quality-of-life issues and believe that a thriving arts community is an asset to Fayetteville. The clinic has enthusiastically supported the arts by sponsoring productions at the Cape Fear Regional Theater, as well as by contributing to the North Carolina Symphony and the Fayetteville Museum of Art.

The clinic's altruism extends well beyond the limits of Fayetteville. One of the physicians, Dr. Stanley Gilbert, participates annually in a program that brings medical care to remote villages of Bolivia. Each summer, Dr. Gilbert and other physicians spend two weeks in small Bolivian villages, where they attend to the medical needs of people whose access to medical care is very limited.

The Cape Fear Orthopaedic Clinic meets specific medical needs with the highest level of professionalism, making it an asset to Fayetteville.

INTERIM HEALTHCARE OF THE EASTERN CAROLINAS, INC.

Interim HealthCare of the Eastern Carolinas, Inc., is a home health-care agency that had its beginnings in Fayetteville. With offices in 12 North Carolina communities, as well as in Myrtle Beach, South Carolina, Interim HealthCare meets the growing need for professional home care at the lowest possible cost.

Licensed and Medicare-certified as a home health agency, Interim HealthCare offers professional nursing services to patients in their residences or in health-care facilities. Among its employees are registered nurses, physical therapists, speech therapists, medical social workers, and home health aides, all of whom are available for intermittent patient visits. All Interim HealthCare employees are screened, reference-checked, and interviewed.

Interim HealthCare also provides supplemental staffing for health-care facilities, using a skill-matching system that provides exactly the right employee for a specific need.

Guided by a formal, written code of ethics, Interim HealthCare recognizes the importance of providing high-quality care not only for patients but for the greater community. Interim HealthCare is Accredited with Commendation by the Joint Commission on Accreditation of Healthcare Organizations.

Among the more technical services Interim HealthCare offers are intravenous therapy and an electronic home monitoring service, known as Interim InTouch, which provides homebound patients with safety, security, and companionship.

Realizing that medical care needs don't always happen on a predictable schedule, Interim HealthCare is an around-the-calendar, around-the-clock operation. A client service representative and a registered nurse are always available by phone to help the company's clients.

Interim HealthCare extends its concern for health care beyond its corporate boundaries. The president of the company, Stephen M. Smith, M.P.H., is the chairman of Health Care '99, an initiative in which the Fayetteville Chamber of Commerce is an active participant. HC99 is intended to strengthen all aspects of health care, and access to it, for the people who live in the nine-county region surrounding Fayetteville. Interim HealthCare associates are encouraged to be actively involved in civic and professional activities at local, regional, state, and national levels.

Interim HealthCare is more than just a successful regional business. It is a concerned corporate citizen as well. The company will continue to make life better for thousands of people as the new century brings new developments and opportunities to Fayetteville.

Carolina Regional Radiology was established in Fayetteville in 1956 by Dr. Hubert Batten, a local radiologist. In the intervening years, as Fayetteville grew and developed, so did the practice, which now provides the medical services of 20 radiologists. Many of these radiologists not only are board-certified but trained in a specialty of radiology, which has become a much more sophisticated area of medicine with the development of magnetic resonance imaging, interventional radiology, and other technological enhancements. No longer does radiology mean only X-rays.

Truly a regional company, Carolina Regional Radiology provides radiology services at Highsmith-Rainey Memorial Hospital, Cape Fear Valley Medical Center, Fayetteville Diagnostic Center, Betsy Johnson Memorial Hospital in Dunn, Columbus County Hospital in Whiteville, and Bladen County Hospital in Elizabethtown. Interpretive services are also provided to the medical clinic at Pope Air Force Base and at Fort Bragg's Womack Army Medical Center, as well as at area physicians' offices and clinics.

Carolina Regional Radiology has been an active participant in Health Care '99, the initiative to provide better access to health care for the people of the Fayetteville region. The practice is also at the forefront of the effort to make women aware of the benefits of mammography. Committed to meeting all the radiological needs of the community, the practice includes not only the traditional diagnostic applications of radiology but also interventional radiology, as used in angioplasty, carotid artery surgery, and neuroradiology.

Like many of Fayetteville's health-care providers, Carolina Regional Radiology recruits professionals to join the practice. Barbara Adcock, the administrator of Carolina Regional Radiology, points out that Fayetteville has become increasingly easy to "sell" to physicians and other health-care professionals.

"The economy is solid," she says. "And that's important for health-care professionals to know. The economic foundation that the military presence provides far outweighs any misapprehensions that people may have about Fayetteville being a military town."

Carolina Regional Radiology has contributed actively to Fayetteville's enhanced quality of life. The group has supported the arts in Fayetteville by contributing to the Cape Fear Regional Theater and the Arts Council of Fayetteville and Cumberland County and by supporting the development of Fayetteville's Botanical Garden and the local public radio station, WFSS.

The group is supportive of efforts to educate the public about sickle cell anemia and highly committed to Fayetteville's CARE clinic, which provides medical care to the segment of the population that has limited access to health care. Several of Carolina Regional Radiology's physicians volunteer their services on behalf of this worthy cause.

Carolina Regional Radiology hires interns from Fayetteville Technical Community College whenever possible, providing local students with hands-on experience in the world of medicine. The physicians of Carolina Regional Radiology also visit local high schools and colleges to encourage interested students in pursuing a career in medicine.

The future of Carolina Regional Radiology includes making every effort to provide access to high-quality radiological services to the region's outlying areas, while maintaining its commitment to Fayetteville. As the twenty-first century approaches, Carolina Regional Radiology is prepared to meet the challenges of providing the best possible radiological services to the people of Fayetteville and the surrounding region.

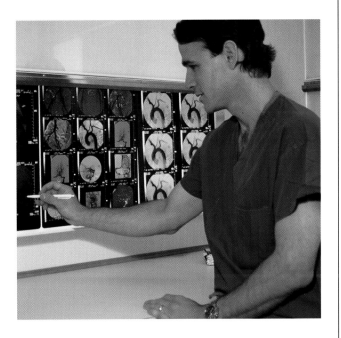

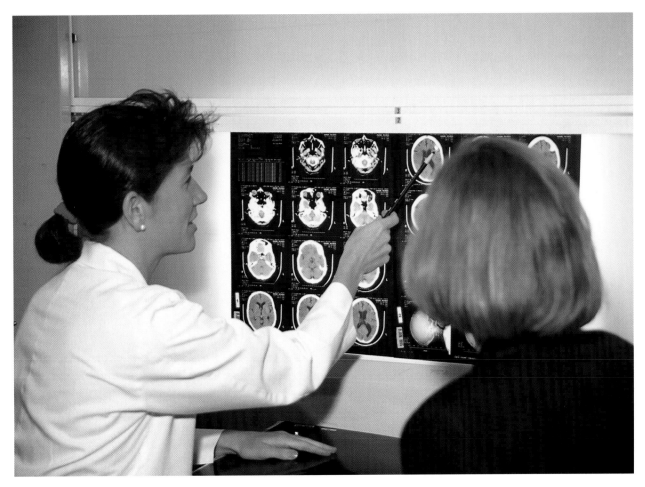

ACKNOWLEDGMENTS

Each of the following corporate profile companies made a valuable contribution to this project. Longstreet Press gratefully acknowledges their participation.

Adia Personnel Services
American Carpets and Interiors
American Uniform Sales, Inc.
Belk
Branch Banking and Trust
Briggs and Sons Tire
Butler's Electric Supply of Fayetteville
Cablevision of Fayetteville
Campbell University
Cape Fear Orthopaedic Clinic
Cape Fear Supply/Comtech, Inc.
Cape Fear Valley Medical Center
Carolina Regional Radiology
Cashwell Appliance Parts, Inc.
Cellular One
Consumers Title Company, Inc.
The Cooking Connection
Cross Creek Mall
CTS Cleaning Systems, Inc.
Cumberland Community Foundation
Cumberland County Public Library
Cutler-Hammer
Fasco Consumer Products, Inc.
Fayetteville Area Economic Development Corporation
Fayetteville Chamber of Commerce
Fayetteville Museum of Art
Fayetteville Publishing Company
Fayetteville State University
Fayetteville Technical Community College
Fayetteville Veterans Affairs Medical Center
First Union National Bank
Healy Wholesale, Inc.
Highsmith-Rainey Memorial Hospital
Home Federal Savings and Loan Association
Hutchens & Senter
Inacomp Computer Center
Interim HealthCare of the Eastern Carolinas, Inc.
James B. Dennis Veterans of Foreign Wars Post 6018
The LSV Partnership
Marvin Allan Door Company, Inc.
Methodist College
Mid-South Insurance Company
Moonlight Communications
North Carolina Communications, Inc.
North Carolina Natural Gas Corporation
Olde Fayetteville Association
PHP, Inc.
Physicians' Total Rehab
PI, Inc.
Powers-Swain Chevrolet-Geo

Prudential John Koenig, REALTORS®
The Public Works Commission
Radisson Prince Charles Hotel
Ramada Inn
Ratley Construction Company, Inc.
Rogers and Breece Funeral Home
Smith Advertising & Associates
Smith Barney
Sprint/Carolina Telephone
Swayn G. Hamlet & Associates, Inc.
Townsend Real Estate
Village Surgical Associates
Weaver Development Company, Inc.
Womack Army Medical Center
WZFX
Yarborough and Hancox, Attorneys at Law

This book was published in cooperation with the Fayetteville Chamber of Commerce and would not have been possible without the support of its members. Longstreet Press is especially grateful to the following individuals for their commitment and for their continued assistance:

Johnny L. Dawkins, Chair, 1995
Fayetteville Chamber of Commerce

Calvin B. Wells, Chair, 1994
Fayetteville Chamber of Commerce

Linda Lee Allan, Vice-Chair, Community Development, 1995
Fayetteville Chamber of Commerce

H. Terry Hutchens, Vice-Chair, Community Development, 1994
Fayetteville Chamber of Commerce

Lynn Carraway, Chair, Marketing Committee,
Community Development
Fayetteville Chamber of Commerce

Glenda S. Margerum, Vice President, Community Development
Fayetteville Chamber of Commerce

The Fayetteville ADvocates
Fayetteville Chamber of Commerce
(Al Cain, Cain & Cain)
(Greg Hathaway, Hathaway & Crawford)
(Jean Hodges, Hodges Associates)
(Gary T. Smith, Smith Advertising & Associates)

Moonlight Communications
(Pat Wright and Jan Johnson)

Dr. William T. Brown
Member, Board of Governors, University of North Carolina

INDEX TO ENTERPRISE SECTION

INDEX TO TEXT